Writing in-Between

Writing in-Between lies at intersections: between theory and praxis; between fiction and non-fiction; between author and reader; between the personal and the political. Beginning with a conceptual glossary that prepares readers for their journey through the book, Dinesh offers two central texts to invite readers to become co-creators. The first, *F for* _____, is written as an academic novella and culminates with an interactive section that is composed of guided invitations for the reader/co-creator. The second text, *Julys*, takes the form of a dramatic memoir and intersperses invitations for readers/co-creators between each of its chapters. Dinesh brings these threads together in an entirely interactive concluding chapter, where her hopes for collaborative meaning making take centre stage. In all of its unique invitations to engage, Dinesh's readers/co-creators can either choose to craft their creations in personal notebooks or blank spaces in this work's physical copy, or to engage more publicly via virtual forums that can be accessed via QR codes and accompanying links that are scattered throughout the book. Guided by questions about writing can do—questions that have shaped Dinesh's work as an artist, scholar, and educator for almost two decades—*Writing in-Between* embodies one central tenet: that the significance of performative writing might be most powerfully experienced through a collaborative process of meaning making between a text's author and its readers turned co-creators.

Nandita Dinesh is Dean of Academic Administration at Mount Tamalpais College, serving incarcerated students inside San Quentin State Prison.

Routledge Focus on Literature

Trauma, Memory and Silence of the Irish Woman in Contemporary Literature
Wounds of the Body and the Soul
Edited by Madalina Armie and Verónica Membrive

Rilke's Hands
An Essay on Gentleness
Harold Schweizer

Orality, Form, and Lyric Unity
Poetics of Michael Donaghy and Don Paterson
Beverley Nadin

Milton and Music
Seth Herbst

Forensic Storytelling and the Literary Roots of Early Modern Feminism
ReSisters
Barbara Abrams

Supernatural Creatures in Arabic Literary Tradition
Ahmed Al-Rawi

Writing in-Between
Collaborative Meaning Making in Performative Writing
Nandita Dinesh

For more information about this series, please visit: www.routledge.com/Routledge-Focus-on-Literature/book-series/RFLT

Writing in-Between
Collaborative Meaning Making in Performative Writing

Nandita Dinesh

Routledge
Taylor & Francis Group
NEW YORK AND LONDON

First published 2024
by Routledge
605 Third Avenue, New York, NY 10158

and by Routledge
4 Park Square, Milton Park, Abingdon, Oxon, OX14 4RN

Routledge is an imprint of the Taylor & Francis Group, an informa business

ISBN: 978-1-032-68580-9 (hbk)
ISBN: 978-1-032-68581-6 (pbk)
ISBN: 978-1-032-68582-3 (ebk)

DOI: 10.4324/9781032685823

Typeset in Times New Roman
by Apex CoVantage, LLC

Contents

Section 1

Between writing and me

I write in between spaces.

I have always written somewhere in between: between theory and practice; between ethnography and autoethnography; between fiction and non-fiction. My first book, *Theatre & War* (2016), took the approach of interspersing more traditionally academic writing with autoethnographic field notes. The *Memos from a Theatre Lab* series (2017, 2018, 2019) used qualitative data analyses from experiments with my students toward better understanding immersive theatre. *Chronicles from Kashmir* (2020) drew on years of theatre-centred undertakings in Kashmir to craft a multimedia, annotated script for a twenty-four-hour immersive performance. Perhaps unsurprisingly then, this book is an extension of concepts that have underscored my work for almost two decades: experimenting in the spaces between form and content; blurring the boundaries between creator and spectator; deepening an understanding of what lies between the personal and the political. There is an additional question in these pages, though; an interrogation that, while consistently examined in my theatre making through a range of participatory aesthetics, has thus far been less explored in my writing: what might it mean for a text to rearticulate the ways in which meaning is collaboratively constructed between author and audience? In writing a book like this one, I want to ask what we might uncover together: me, the person who has started this book, and you, the reader who will be invited to extend it. Perhaps the significance of in-between writing might be enriched not via authorial assertions, but through messy, collaborative, unpredictable conversations between all those who choose to engage with it.

There are two sections that form the crux of this book. The first, **In between the political and the personal: *F for*_____**, is a creation

DOI: 10.4324/9781032685823-1

that arose when news around the world spoke of children being held in detention centres in the United States. Written as an academic novella, *F for _____* culminates with an interactive component in which you—the reader, the co-creator—will be invited to partner on the generation of content. The second section, **In between the personal and the political: *Julys,*** has been written in the form of a dramatic memoir and integrates invitations for collaboratio n. You can contribute your voice by writing in the blank spaces in the printed book, or by using the QR codes and their accompanying links to share your work on this book's online portal.

Before moving on to the texts themselves, though:

A glossary

> Language is also a place of struggle.
> [We] struggle in language to recover ourselves, to reconcile, to reunite, to renew.
> Our words are not without meaning, they are an action, a resistance.
> Language is also a place of struggle.
>
> bell hooks (2014, p. 160)

The writing in this book is shaped by my particular use of language, and I don't simply mean the predominant use of English. In the spirit of ensuring that you—my collaborative meaning maker—are better positioned to understand/ contextualize/ engage with the tongues in which I speak, I draw inspiration from Ronald J Pelias' (2014) *An Alphabet of Performative Writing* to offer you a curated glossary of terms and concepts that shape the words in these pages:

- **Performative writing**
  Della Pollock (1998) offers six possible characteristics that might constitute performative writing; a text's ability to be "evocative," "metonymic," "subjective," "citational," "nervous," and "consequential." Not sure what that means? Neither did I, till I came across a text that seemed to embody—and extend—the concepts Pollock puts forward: Sarah Kane's (2015) *4.48 Psychosis*. Written as a text that does not name a single character and contains blank spaces, series of numbers, descriptions of hallucinations, and analytical accounts of medical diagnoses, *4.48 Psychosis* was an "aha"

moment for me. Kane helped me gain my own understanding of what performative writing might be: texts in which form performs content; texts in which the visual shape of the words on the page—in conjunction with specifically chosen textual forms of communication (prescriptions, recipes, letters, for example)—might catalyze new layers of meaning to what writing can do to its reader.

- **Autoethnography**
  My doctoral undertaking involved a multi-year investigation into the collaborative creation of dramatic representations about/from Kashmir, integrating perspectives and voices from stakeholders who often do not exist in the same dialogic space (civilians, government forces, and militants). There were many ethical complexities to this endeavour, especially as an Indian woman seeking to create in Kashmir/with Kashmiris, and I found grounding in the work of Norman K. Denzin (2003, 2009) and the insights he offers vis-à-vis the potential of autoethnography in/through/as performance. Since then, I have often used the term "autoethnography" to frame how I write about contexts that I do not have the lived experience of. I use the interpretive and subjective methods of autoethnography in order to

  - remind the reader of the biases that I bring to my writing
  - disavow any appearance of expertise about matters I am a student of
  - transparently showcase the discomfort that might be (and, perhaps, should be) experienced when writing about others' lives

  And yes, I absolutely recognize—and constantly grapple with—the potential for unfettered self-indulgence that can arise when an autoethnographic focus on the "I" is used to foster understanding of an Other.
- **Positioning**
  Insider-Outsider |Outsider-Insider |Personal-Political | Political-Personal.

  What does it mean to write about experiences that I have not lived? How can I use my lived experience to understand the lives of others in a way that does the *least* harm? What are formal elements that might address complex political and social phenomena without risking being reductive or sensational? Like much of my other writing, especially *Chronicles from Kashmir* (2020), questions about authorial positioning consume *F for _____* and *Julys*.

- **Collaborative meaning making**
  Devised theatre is the point of departure for my understanding of collaborative meaning making. A form of creation in which scripts/performances are generated from/with the people in the room to devise theatre means to incorporate exercises that introduce stimuli, which then evoke creative responses through writing, song, dance, or drama. In this way, devised theatre can resemble pedagogies of active learning and experiential education—the process is as important as the product; traditional power dynamics are challenged between director and actor, between teacher and student; each creator in the ensemble of a devised performance adds to the meaning that is made in/from it.

  Devised theatre works often ask audiences to let go of more expected modes of spectatorship, and the nature of such invitations can take myriad forms: from the direct problem-solving spectactor in Augusto Boal's (1974) *Theatre of the Oppressed*, to the less obvious strategies that Bertolt Brecht (1968) uses to invite critical—non-emotionally indulgent—empathy; to the experiential approach of spectator participation that is used by Griselda Gambaro (1992) in *Information for Foreigners* to invite spectators to question our own culpability in acts of violence. How might such notions of collaborative creation and participation, so present in devised theatre, be extended to the meaning making experience of a book?
- **Decolonizing the mind**
  Language as a site of resistance—as a space to explore "decolonising the mind"—is central to how I think about writing. Encountering Ngũgĩ wa Thiong'o (1992) was the first time I contended with the various hegemonies that pervade my writing: those that come from having grown up in southern India with English as my first language; those that were learned through having to write and rewrite, verbatim, lines from school textbooks; those that I imbibed as a graduate student who found much of academic writing to be alienating and elitist and yet, felt the need to replicate. It would be hyperbolic (and disingenuous) to claim that *Writing in Between* accomplishes anything close to the kind of intellectual decolonization that Thiong'o calls for. Instead, I will say that this book is simply one more effort in my repertoire; one more step toward growing a more robust understanding of what it might mean to decolonize my writing.

- **The two texts**

  Academic novella

  "This is not really a novel, right? It's too . . . academic?" a student asked, about a decade ago, while we studied Manuel Puig's (2010) *Kiss of the Spider Woman.* Although I didn't know how to answer my student's question all that eloquently at the time, now, years later, I would invite them to consider Puig's work as an academic novel: a text that uses a fictional frame to dig into theoretical questions emerging from socio-political phenomena in Argentina at the time. For Puig, in *Kiss of the Spider Woman*, aesthetics typically assigned to scholarship are primarily visible in extensive footnotes that feature discourses surrounding sexuality, film theory, and Marxism. For me, in *F for* _____, formal devices usually ascribed to works of fiction are used to explore debates in the realms of immigration, sexuality, and allyship. When I call *F for* _____ an academic novella, I do not use it as a prescriptive term with a particular genesis; neither am I suggesting that academic texts and novellas are always absent of the others' traits. I offer the term only as a way to capture the particular kind of in-betweenness that *F for*_____ embodies.

  Dramatic memoir

  I use the term "dramatic memoir" in the same spirit as I do "academic novella"—to highlight the in-betweenness that *Julys* inhabits in its excavation of autobiographical narratives through formal elements that are usually expected in drama. Resonating with what is sometimes called "autofiction," *Julys* is informed by the desire to use memory as a way to critically reflect on larger forces that shape personal and political identities.

While there is a lot more that I could tell you about each of the abovementioned terms and how each finds its place in *F for* ______ and *Julys*, I shall pause here.

I want the meaning that is made from this book to emerge in conversation between you, me, and every other person who engages with these words.

I want the meaning that is made from these pages to surface through an engagement between all of us.

We write in between spaces.

Works referenced

Boal, A. (1985) *Theatre of the oppressed.* Theatre Communications Group.

Brecht, B. and Willet, J. (1977) *Brecht on theatre: The development of an aesthetic.* Methuen.

Denzin, N.K. (2003) *Performance ethnography: The call to performance.* SAGE Research Methods Online Edition: SAGE.

Denzin, N.K. (2009) 'A critical performance pedagogy that matters', *Ethnography and Education*, 4(3), pp. 255–270.

Dinesh, N. (2016) *Theatre and war.* Open Book Publishers.

Dinesh, N. (2017) *Memos from a theatre lab: Exploring what immersive theatre 'does'.* Routledge.

Dinesh, N. (2018) *Memos from a theatre lab: Spaces, relationships, and immersive theatre.* Vernon Press.

Dinesh, N. (2019) *Memos from a theatre lab: Immersive theatre & time.* Vernon Press.

Dinesh, N. (2020) *Chronicles from Kashmir: An annotated, multimedia script.* Open Book Publishers.

Gambaro, G. (1992) *Information for foreigners: Three plays.* Northwestern University Press.

hooks, bell. (2014) *Yearning: Race, gender, and cultural politics.* Routledge.

Kane, S. (2015) *4.48 psychosis.* Methuen.

Pelias, R.J. (2016) *Performance.* Routledge.

Pollock, D. (1998) 'Performing writing', in *The ends of performance.* New York University Press, pp. 73–103.

Puig, M. (2010) *Kiss of the spider woman.* Vintage.

wa Thiong'o, N. (1986) *Decolonizing the mind: The politics of language in African literature.* J. Currey.

Section 2

Between the political and the personal

F for ________

1 F for (not just about) food

Chikki,

Here's the recipe you asked for.

Mutton biriyani

Ingredients

- meat: half kg
- rice: one cup
- tomatoes: five
- onions: three
- ginger garlic paste: one tsp
- turmeric powder: half tsp
- chilli powder: one tsp
- patta: one small piece
- grambu: four
- elakka: three
- a small piece of bay leaf or biriyani leaf
- pudina leaves: quarter cup

To grind together

- coconut: quarter (grated)
- cashew nuts: ten

Method

- cook the rice
- chop onions. fry the onions in a frying pan with a little oil till golden brown

DOI: 10.4324/9781032685823-3

- add chilli powder, turmeric powder, and then the ginger garlic paste
- fry till the raw smell goes (adding little water)
- add the cleaned meat pieces to it
- fry till it becomes nice and brown
- then add the chopped tomatoes, pudina, and ground coriander
- close the pan and keep it closed for a while
- put 1 tsp salt and transfer the ingredients to a pressure cooker
- add 1 cup water and leave it to cook for ten minutes (after the sound comes)
- after the meat is cooked, add the coconut-cashew nut paste into the mix and remove and keep aside
- in the pressure cooker, add ghee
- fry patta, grambu, elakka, and bay leaf
- add rice and fry for a minute
- add two cups of water and one tsp salt and cook well
- after the water is fully dry, add the meat preparation
- mix well and serve hot

Heed my warning: this dish is a different beast.

If you really want that extra zing, you can't juggadofy a single step! The more attention you give to the exact consistency of the rice and the blending of the spices, the more care you give to the ways in which the flavours and the textures come into contact with each other, the more time you give to the marination of the meat and its eventual entrance into the cooker, the better the biriyani. This dish needs time. It needs tenderness. Like most of our delicacies, there are multitudinous layers . . . so many versions of its history, so many interactions of its ingredients, so many stages to its coming together.

I don't think I've asked you this yet, but did you discover this love for cooking at the same time that we got back in touch? From my calculations, there must have been at least a few years in between the time when you moved there and when you realized that you had this interest, right? Had you had started cooking before or after you thought to get back in touch? I ask because I don't think I remember how exactly it happened. How the "I-won't-learn-how-to-cook-because-all-women-from-this-country-don't-need-to-know-how-to-cook" S_ blossomed into a chef who whips up delicacies in foreign lands!

Anyway.

I'm continuing to make my list of cities and creating a pros and cons list for each of them. It's the big cities that are drawing me in. Metros in which I can have my space. Bustling places where the odds are higher of being able to find others like me to openly create community with.

I do consider leaving the county fairly often, but when push comes to shove, I cannot stand the thought. I don't know how you did it. I know why you did it. Why you felt you had to leave. But I just can't bring myself to think about that option seriously. Every time I come close to it, something happens. I'll eat a particularly delicious kulfi in the afternoon sunshine. Or I'll meet a lovely uncle at the chai stall, who doesn't seem to care that I'm enjoying my cigarette as much as he is. Or I'll be in an auto and my latest favourite song will start playing on the radio. Or I'll read something that just scratches the surface of a cultural complexity that one could spend multiple lifetimes trying to understand.

I don't think I used to be this sentimental about the motherland. Was I? Back then? I can't remember if I've always been like this, or if this is a new dimension to who I have become. I distinctly remember only wanting to eat continental food from the college buffet line. I remember rolling my eyes when they'd force us to sing the national anthem every Friday afternoon. I remember being frustrated when they'd shove a particular idea of "this is our culture" down our throats. A culture that wouldn't allow us to do this or that. A culture that wouldn't allow us to be this or that. A culture that we were forced to adhere to, in order to be accepted.

Maybe that hasn't changed.

Maybe what's changed is that I have come to see so many exceptions to the rule. So many people who don't accept claustrophobic, immovable definitions of belonging to this vast, infinite place. So many kindred spirits who are genuinely trying to evolve the collective's understanding of what it means to be from here. So many of these so many that we cannot be exceptions anymore. So many so-many-s who are writing our own rules about what it means to embody the cultures of these devastating geographies.

I ask how you remember me because in my version of events, these shifts in my understanding of place and home and culture and belonging can be traced back to that year. That year with a capital T. To those months of needing to get away after your wedding. The months that forced me to travel to nooks and crannies that I would never have even attempted to reach had my feet not kept moving to keep the anguish at bay. Months of aimless wandering that led to epiphany-inducing encounters with different versions of this land, each one of which helped me hope again. Hope that there exists a version of this nation in which I can love and be loved. Warmly. Welcomingly. Openly. Without rancour. Or shame. Or fear.

I'm re-evaluating so much, and as I do, it's impossible to ignore how we've used these letters to talk without talking. I want to talk about that time.

I want to talk.
I want to listen.
I want to know your side of the story.
I wasn't ready before.
I think I am now.
Maybe you are too?

F_

2 Interview one

A_ Thanks for doing this with me.

When A_ first told her mother that she wanted to interview her, S_ had wanted to turn her daughter down. S_ knew that the interview, simply by virtue of her relationship to the theme—not to mention the interviewer—would likely become intimate. Personal. Intense. Qualities that could never be used to describe the kinds of conversations that S_ had had with A_ until this day. But, if the last few months had taught them anything, it was that S_ wanted to—needed to—redefine her relationship with A_. She wanted to try and have an intimate, personal conversation with her daughter so that they might have the slightest chance of repairing their relationship. This mother wants to have a new kind of conversation with her offspring so that she might redeem herself. S_ wants to try and have this conversation with A_ because she feels like it is time for the younger woman to learn more. More about her place in this. All of this.

A_ So I just want to reassure you that I won't ask anything about . . . you know. This is more . . . more about your own thoughts, as an immigrant to this country, about what you think about . . . you know . . . like . . . everything that's going on. So . . . I just wanted to, like, put that out there.

Externally, S_ reassures A_ that there are no questions that are off limits. Within herself though, she heaves a sigh of relief. S_ does not want to talk about matters that she is only now beginning to learn how to articulate. The last thing S_ wants to do is talk about her inner tumults with A_; the turmoil that had thrown all their lives into disarray.

DOI: 10.4324/9781032685823-4

So, even though S_ reassures her daughter that any questions could be asked in the context of this conversation, she doesn't really mean it.

A_ I realized the other day that I've never asked you, directly, what you think of the detention centres. So, I think . . . like . . . I think we should start there . . . if that's too general a question I can be more specific? OK. So . . . As someone who also came to this country as an immigrant, when you see others who share a similar condition as yours land up in very, very different circumstances, what do you think your role is in trying to . . . like . . . you know . . . to address that situation?

S_ is honest with A_ in a way that she has never been before. S_ tells her how, until everything with F_ had happened, she had never given much thought to anything that she could/should be doing for/about those who shared the same label of "immigrant." How radically her attitude toward questions of immigration and detention and asylum seeking have gained a newfound significance in the last few months. Somewhat like the final stages of cake making, where the mixture almost seamlessly glides off the sides of the pan that contains it, S_ finds the inner texture that she needs to share her fears about F_'s silence. She tells A_ about the nightmares she has been having. That F_ is now just one more detained immigrant lost inside a system that S_ wishes she knew more about.

S_ reveals to A_ that she has been—is—plagued by guilt. Guilt for surviving. Guilt for thriving. Guilt for having had a relatively simple immigration process. Guilt for not having been detained or deported. Guilt for having had the easy path. Guilt for having come of out of all of it alive. Guilt for not having done more to protect F_ from the fate S_ was sure had befallen her. Guilt. Guilt. Guilt. Guilt. That's all S_ can feel now, she tells her daughter, and she does not know what she needs to do to transform it.

S_ I want to . . . If it's OK with you, darling, I would love to be more involved in the Safar that you're designing with your father . . . beyond this interview, I mean . . . I . . . I need to feel something other than guilt, and I think that by helping you . . . you know . . . maybe by working on something like this . . . I can learn some things about how the system works and . . . I don't know. I just need to find a different way to think about . . . everything.

A_ Of course. You can be part of this process as much as you want, ma. You can even come to some of the interviews I've set up, if you would like? It would be a nice way for us to spend some, like, quality time together.

Silence.

S_ I would love that. OK, chalo, sorry, continue. I interrupted you. What's the next question?

A_ No—yeah . . . so the second question I have for you is about, like, your idea of home . . . What does home mean to you, and how has that idea changed over the years?

S_ looks down at her hands for a long while before she answers this one. She knows that what she is about to say is probably not what A_ wants to, or expects to, hear. S_ knows that A_ expects to hear some version of the well-known trope. Some version of the notion that an immigrant's understanding of home has no choice but to shift because of the new country that has become their primary place of residence. But S_ tells A_, this has never been the case for her. For S_, home has always meant one place: the country in which she had been born. The country to which, she hopes, she will return when it is time for her to die. Home, for S_, has always been that place. Even though new lands and peoples and cultures and foods and families had come into her life and shaped aspects of who she has now become—aspects of herself that she doesn't always dislike—S_ has never found another home. Home has always been where she had grown up. Home has always been a particular set of geographies and histories and gastronomies. Even if she only got to be there, physically, for a few days a year, that is home. It turns out that, for S_ anyway, home can be divorced from physical presence. It turns out that home can be found in distance. In absence. In loss.

A_ But . . . if . . . if you've never felt like this is your home . . . like . . . do you think that . . . if . . . you know . . . like . . . if I wasn't part of the . . . if you hadn't had me . . . do you think you still would have continued to stay here? Or would have gone back?

S_ can see the genuine concern in A_'s eyes. She can also see the fear. The guilt. A_'s guilt for being the one of the reasons her mother didn't have any choice but to remain in this country. S_ can see A_'s dis-ease. She can see her impassioned curiosity. And in this moment, S_ knows that she has one of two choices. She could lie. S_ could lie and tell her daughter that there is nothing she regrets, and that A_'s existence has never prevented her from doing anything that she would/would not have done in her absence. S_ could lie and tell A_ that even though this place has never felt like home, she had found home in A_. Creating elaborately concocted lies is one way for S_ to answer A_'s question. The other choice is for S_ to do something that she is only now learning to. She could choose to be honest. Brutally honest. The kind of honesty that can feel like physical suffocation. The kind of honesty that can sting and burn and corrode. The kind of honesty that most claim they desire, but that very few can endure. The kind of honesty that mothers are not supposed to inflict on their children.

S_ could choose to tell the truth, look her daughter in the eye, and say "yes." Yes. Yes, if she had not had a child, yes, she would have probably returned home as soon as she possibly could have. If S_ had not had A_, she probably would not have stayed here: in the country, in the marriage. If not for the fact that she gave birth to a child, S_ would have likely returned to the only home she has ever known. That is the truth. That is S_'s brutal truth. That is the physically-suffocating truth that S_ can choose to tell in this moment, with the simple hope that A_ will be able to understand. Understand complexity. Understand nuance. Understand that this kind of hypothetical isn't simply a choice between this or that. That this kind of hypothetical is constructed around a life that has veered so off course that its liver might never again be able to recognize a path that isn't the one she is already on.

These are her choices as S_ sees it: the concocted lie or suffocating veracity.

S_ chooses to speak her truth.

The kind of truth that mothers are not supposed to speak to their daughters.

The kind of truth that mothers are not supposed to speak to themselves.

The kind of truth that defiles a glorified belief that there is nothing more noble than bearing and raising children.

A_ Wow.
I didn't expect—no, no. Don't. You don't have to explain anything.
I think I always knew that . . .
I think, somewhere, like, I always felt that. That if not for me, you would have . . . seriously, don't apologize. I'm actually really glad you decided to just tell me the truth. Really. I . . .
I'm glad you told me.
I'm glad I know.

Mother and daughter have no choice but to share a moment of silence. To sit in camaraderie like they never had before, and to simply consider the other.

Luckily for S_, A_ has not only become a young woman who can handle complexity, she craves it.

Luckily for A_, S_ has become someone who sees the value in truth-telling, however gnarly the nature of that telling might be.

Luckily, in a serendipitous coming together of nature and nurture, mother and daughter feel like they can just be in the presence of the other. Just, be. No strings attached.

Silence.

A_ . . . I was wondering . . . if you have time now . . . can you . . . you know that pudding that you make? Refrigerator pudding? Will you teach me how to make it?

S_ Seriously?

A_ Yeah. I was craving it the other day and . . . can we make some now?

As S_ looks for the ingredients to make the pudding her daughter wants, her heart is full. This is another first in their relationship: the first time A_ had ever asked S_ to teach her how to make any kind of food. If that isn't enough, S_ is particularly struck by her daughter's choice. That of all the complicated dishes that she has made for A_ over the years, her daughter chooses the simple dessert that is made from biscuits and cocoa powder and brandy and sugar and cashews and served with a dollop of heavy cream. S_ is overcome. That of all the dishes that this mother has made her daughter over the years, A_ chooses the dessert that is inextricably linked to the last time S_ and F_ saw each other.

It feels like the universe is telling S_ something. The kind of something that makes her slightly hopeful for her disappeared more-than-friend. The kind of something that makes her realize that her daughter will always, inexplicably, remind S_ of a woman from another lifetime. The kind of something that has S_ stuck somewhere between bemusement and grief: bemusement for all the ways in which F_ remains present in her life; grief for all the ways in which she doesn't.

F_ had made refrigerator pudding that night, all those years ago, to celebrate the first few pages of a novel that S_ was working on. It was a simple gesture. A dessert that was meant to mark the beginning of S_'s artistic journey; the culinary articulation of an affection that only one of them knew to recognize. Somehow, over sugar-induced joy and the adrenaline that can come only from the act of creating something from nothing, S_ can still remember the moment she realized that this night was going to be different. That this night was going to be the kind of night that changed everything she thought she understood about herself. It was a simple moment. A beautifully simple moment in which F_ reached over to gently wipe cream from the corner of S_'s mouth. A split second.

A_ Let me know when you're ready to get started?

3 Safar

Part one

A Witness walks into the Safar.

They sit behind a glass wall. The kind where they can see in, but the Detainees and the Officers behind the glass cannot see out.

If the Witness pays attention, they will find a lot to see/ notice/ feel/ analyze/ deconstruct/ perceive/ consider/ internalize/ reflect on/ debate/ digest. But they can just as well decide to ignore/ ridicule/ disengage/ space out/ distance/ support/ reinforce/ perpetuate/ solidify/ resign.

It is up to them.

-f-f-f-f-f-f-f-f-f-f-f-f-f-

"Wake up"

The Witness might choose to watch a doctor-turned-Detainee who is rolling out of their bed, or making their bed, or brushing their teeth on the sink that's near the bed, or washing their face in the sink that's near the bed, or taking a piss or shit on the toilet that's near their bed.

The Witness might choose to watch a mother-turned-Detainee who is in solitary confinement. Alone because she has broken a rule that she does not understand. Alone because she has broken a rule that she cannot understand. Alone because she has broken a rule that she chose not to understand.

The Witness might choose to watch an Officer who believes they are serving a greater good and is watching all of the Detainees through the slivers of glass on their cell doors. An Officer who then takes care of an interminable amount of paperwork, or shoots the shit with another Officer, temporarily forgetting that their job entails watching

DOI: 10.4324/9781032685823-5

the Detainees. An Officer who is then called away on an emergency because a Detainee—somewhere else in the detention facility—has been seen harming themselves. An Officer who is called away on an emergency because a Detainee—somewhere else in the detention facility—has been seen harming another Detainee. An Officer who is called away on an emergency because a Detainee—somewhere else in the detention facility—has been seen harming an Officer.

The Witness might choose to watch the carefully designed environment: the windowless-ness of the rooms, the ever-present fluorescent lighting, the monochromatic walls and floors and ceilings and furniture and clothes, the bleach that is eating through every surface in the facility, the cameras that are watching the Witness watch the Officers watching the Detained, the cameras that are watching the Witness watch the Detained who are watching the Officers, the cameras that are watching the Watchers and the Watched with an indiscriminate gaze.

The Witness might choose to watch a Detainee like F_ who has been discriminated against in their country of birth, in their home, for being a way that does not conform with that society's understanding of what it means to be part of it. A Detainee who finds themselves in circumstances under which they fear for their lives; a situation in which continuing to live in their country of origin is no longer tenable. Where there is a certifiable risk of death or some other form of decapitation.

-f-f-f-f-f-f-f-f-f-f-f-f-f-

"COUNT"

The Detainees are counted by the Officers with support from the cameras.

One

Two

Three

Four

. . .

. . .

. . .

. . .

. . .

Until the registered number of Detainees is confirmed as being present and accounted for.

This can take a while.

-f-f-f-f-f-f-f-f-f-f-f-f-f-

4 F for fierce

Chiks,

Sorry about the long silence. The move happened. I love this city. My brain has been exploding since I've come here—I don't even know where to begin.

Next time you are in the country, you need to come and meet me here. You need to meet the people I've been working with, living with, being with. You will love them. They will love you.

Ok. First let me give you the channa batoora recipes that you asked for. You might have found a better recipe already (it's been a while, I know) but this one's foolproof (Achamma's, but with some tweaks that Ma has made over the years.) I've also included two channa recipes: the spicy one for you; the not-so-spicy one in case you intend to feed those phirangs this stuff.

Batoora

- half kg maida
- one cup milk
- half cup curd
- one tsp baking soda
- half tsp salt
- one tsp sugar

Directions:

- kozhachu-fy the given ingredients, like you would chapati maavu

DOI: 10.4324/9781032685823-6

- keep in the fridge for two hours, covered
- make small balls of dough
- roll each one into a small circle, while heating the oil
- ensure that the oil is hot enough, drop a small bit of dough in the oil, and it should fluff and rise to the surface
- drop the circles in (as many as will fit the pan)
- keep pressing the batoora down with a spatula so that it rises well
- flip
- around one minute a side if on low heat

Kabuli channa (non-spicy)

- 500 gms kabuli channa
- 100 gms oil
- 100 gms capsicum
- 50 gms green chillies
- 30 gms amchor power
- five gms turmeric powder
- 50 gms coriander powder
- salt to taste

Directions:

- boil the channa and drain
- chop the green chillies finely
- cut the capsicum into medium size pieces
- heat the oil
- add capsicum, green chillies, and sauté
- now add the channa, coriander, amchor powder, and turmeric
- mix well
- keep on fire for five to ten minutes

Spicy channa

- soak the channa overnight and boil
- grind two onions

- heat oil and fry onions with chopped ginger (small piece) until brown
- add beaten curds (1 cup), cloves, cumin seeds, chilli powder (1 tsp), and salt
- add the chickpeas to the curd and fry for 10 minutes
- remove from fire and add 2 tsp amchor powder
- serve hot

It's all felt so serendipitous. A friend of a friend was going to this meeting—a planning meeting—for an event. I didn't even know the specifics of the event till I got there. And then this amazing speaker got up on to the stage and, in just a few minutes, she had every single person in that room fired up, inspired, and raring to go.

I was bowled over as I listened to her speak.

This strong, articulate, incredibly brave woman just blew me away with how magnificently she spoke. To us. About us. With us. There were many things that she said that day that struck me, but the one that felt like a shot to my heart was when she spoke about the need for people like us to be more vocal. The need for us to be proud. The need for us to stand up and speak to who we are. Despite the risks. Because of the risks. Through the risks. "It's only when we stake claim to space," she said, "when we take up space and demand to be heard, that we will even have a fighting chance."

I was so inspired by her, S_, that —you won't believe it.

Are you ready?

Are you sitting down?

<u>I told them.</u>

I know.

I feel like I need to insert a dramatic pause here so that you can absorb the weight of what I just said.

Dramatic pause.

All these years and all it took was hearing fighting words from an inspiring stranger. Not *all* it took. Obviously. I know it's not as simple as that. Clearly, I had to be ready, and it took everything that's happened until this point for me to be able to listen to her in that moment and realize that the time had come. That I wanted to make it the time. Does that make sense? It's almost like I had been waiting for the right time, and her words made me feel like I didn't need to wait. I could make it the time I wanted to be. So I went back for the weekend, booked myself into a hotel, went home for a surprise visit, and told them.

One more d*ramatic pause?*

I told them. Amma. Acha. Achamma. I told them.

And it was hard. It was fucking hard. Silence. Tears. Questions. Accusations. I left after a little while. It was too much. "That's that," I thought as I was leaving. "I'll have to wait years for them to speak to me. If they ever decide to speak to me again." We all know so many whose families have disowned them. Why should mine be any different? But—and I'm still a little in shock about this, I think—they called me a couple of hours later. *They* called *me*, S_. And asked me to come back to the house.

Turns out, it was Achamma's doing. I thought she'd be the one to have the toughest time processing my revelation. But the eighty-year-old woman was the one who looked at my parents after I left and said, "So what?" So. What. Can you believe that? Apparently, my folks had tried to argue with her. Told her that she didn't really understand what I had said. She put my parents in their place, though. "I've watched movies," she said apparently. "They can be nice people."

I know. I know. I'm still taking that as a win, though.

I can breathe easier. Knowing that I can let them in. Show them who I am. Without fear. Without nervousness. That at least within the safe arms of family, I am loved for who I am.

"Do you have a . . . you know . . . special friend?" he asked finally. And when I said no, he had many more questions: "When did you first know? Why did it take you so long to tell us? Have you had any serious relationships?" So I told him about her and how we'd met during my travels after college; how she was the one I had been going to see what I was living at home and would tell them I was going for a drive. You should have seen his face. He was upset, not because I had lied to them at that time or anything like that. No. "I wish you had introduced us to her. You seemed so happy during that period, and we knew it couldn't be only the success with your pop-up restaurants that was making your eyes shine so brightly."

I did not know my parents were these people. I really did not. Makes me think that I should have given them a chance earlier. Learned who they really are, instead of assuming that I knew the kind of people they were likely to be. Maybe everyone deserves that. The chance to show us who they are.

I'm working on them. My fears. My fear of the known. Of the unknown. My fear of taking space. Of claiming it. My fear of being noticed. Of being seen. I've started spending more time with the group (the one that was planning the event I went to—you know why I'm being vague about who they are). It turns out that the speaker who inspired me is really down-to-earth, and open, and over the last month or so, she has become a mentor of sorts. She has lived the story I was always afraid of. Her family disowned her when she came out to them. They kicked her out of the house and to this day, they threw her out almost fifteen years ago, they don't talk to her. Her parents, S_. They've completely stopped speaking to her, and she tells me that it's almost like she doesn't have a biological family anymore.

Instead of being broken by their rejection, though, instead of letting her family's disavowal burn her to ashes, she's allowed their actions to become exquisitely haunting scars that contribute to her fierceness. She wears these scars with something that I can only describe as pride. Like she's telling her family and the world that whatever they do to her, however much their wounds disfigure her, she will transform. Their welts she will wear like tattoos. Their gashes like jewellery. Whatever the world does to her, her transformation will not cease.

Yes, I have a little bit of a crush on her.

Okay, more than a little bit.

She is something else.

I think what makes her so breathtaking to me—I hope you're not uncomfortable with how much I'm gushing—is that her fire shines through despite the fear that she feels. She's not fearless, in that she has no fear. She's fearless because she doesn't let that feeling stop her. In this part of the country, she's a high-profile figure. People are always talking about her in news reports and magazines: those like me, who applaud and admire and thirst for her graceful valour; the many who don't want her (or those like her, like me) to have a voice and hurl threats of violence for what they perceive as her/our role in corrupting and decimating the culture that apparently only they can stake claim to. I worry for her. For her physical safety, I mean. Emotionally, intellectually, psychologically, she might be capable of transforming figurative and metaphorical wounds into badges of honour. But the physical risks that come from her being who she is . . . that's a different minefield all together. How do you transform attacks on your life? I asked her this once, and she just smiled at me. "What's worrying about unknown, unknowable threats going to accomplish?"

From her, these words don't sound like an acquiescence to fate. They feel like a call to battle.

I'm so new to all of this, S_. This is the first time I've been around people who are not only like me, but who are living their lives so differently from the one option I thought I had.

I think that's the part that keeps me awake at night.

I can look at the world now and see options. Options! Suddenly, I can actually see the possibility of different futures. Futures that I can choose from. Futures that I can devour.

I want you to come here and meet some of these people, Chikster. There are people here, in this group, who once were in marriages—both arranged and not—for years, sometimes decades, before they realized that they couldn't live that way anymore. There are folks in this community who have deliberately chosen marriages where neither partner is physically attracted to the other, but between whom there exists a deep and abiding loyalty and friendship; a platonic spouse of the opposite sex who allows them to keep their biological families in their lives, while also creating room for each individual in the union to find different kinds of intimacy in the arms of others. There are those who have camouflage partners, who live double lives; they hide themselves at home but here, when they are with us, in our company, they live their truths. And yes, sometimes, it hurts to witness the weight of this double life that they're living. Sometimes I can feel the weight of the burden that they carry. But I also know that there are some amongst these undercover agents who have found their own version of joy; their own versions of truth; their own acceptance of themselves. Each of the individuals in this amazing group have come to their actualities in different ways, accepted their truths in different ways. I want you to come here and meet some of these people because I think they will do for you, what they have done for me: inspire you to think about the parts of yourself you want to keep and those you might be ready or need to shed.

My life is consumed by questions these days, and I am wandering down lanes of pondering with the hope that, someday soon, I will figure out how to translate abstract thoughts into concrete action. I've spent so long being quiet. So long being invisible. I'm craving visibility. I'm craving a microphone. I'm burning to use my voice. But unlike her, my fear seems to stop me. My fear of the what ifs and maybes. What if I'm loud and have to face verbal and physical and every other kind of assault as a result? Maybe if I'm more visible, the intimidations and aggressions will grow because of a government that does not value my existence? I always thought that the worst kind of government is one that demonizes a segment of its own population. A government that dehumanizes a group because of a particular thing that the majority don't see as being legitimate. Now, though, I think that might be another kind of worst. The kind of worst in which an entire group of people is not even acknowledged as existing. Because if they—we—don't exist, how can we be part of any kind of discourse? If they claim that we don't exist, there is no one to suppress or dehumanize or disappear. If we don't exist, we don't even need to be recognized. At least when individuals are demonized, their existence is acknowledged. They are seen as being. When existences themselves are erased, when we're not even there enough to be demonized, when we're not even seen as being, then what?

How does one deal with absolute and complete erasure?

Anyway. I should probably stop writing now. It's getting late here. Before I do, though, I wanted to quickly say, I know that all these musings might make for less than comfortable reading for you. And a part of me wants to apologize for bringing up things that you might not want to deal with. Please know that if you don't want to deal with the questions or ideas that I'm bringing up, you absolutely do not have to. But I know that this is what I need right now—I need to share what I'm living. What I'm thinking.

If you do want to engage, if you do want to think through the weight you're carrying—we both know that you are—please know that I'm here. That I plan to always be here. In the way that I couldn't be all those years ago.

No expectations.

No demands.

I'm here to share your load, in whatever small way that I can.

Until soon.

F_

5 Interview two

A_ If there was one thing you would want non-immigrants in this country to know about immigrants' experiences trying to build a life here, what would that be?

The surveillance.

Z_ speaks about surveillance. If there is something that he wants a non-immigrant to understand about his life as an immigrant to this country, it is ways in which the immigrant body feels surveilled. Watched. Evaluated. Monitored. From the very first step in the arduous process of applying for the necessary paperwork, the immigrant's experience—Z_ tells A_—is governed by different forms of surveillance. Cameras. Fingerprinting machines. Photographs. Paperwork. Signatures. Search engine results. People.

A_ Thank you for sharing that. I didn't realize that . . . I know there are cameras everywhere in the detention centres, but I didn't think that the surveillance aspect also, like, extended outside the prison into . . . I appreciate your telling me that.

Short pause.

If you were given the chance to help the immigrants who have been placed in detention centres by, like, sponsoring them till their legal status is sorted out—sponsoring usually means, like, hosting people in your home and paying for their costs of living . . . you know, because they can't work and most of the folks . . . like, the clients at the organization where I'm interning, they had to come in illegally so they can't work till things have been sorted

DOI: 10.4324/9781032685823-7

out. So one way to help them is like . . . if they are able to get out on parole . . . for families to take them in and sponsor them . . . until their cases receive, like, the final decision.

Z_ and D_ have overlapping and disagreeing answers to this question.

Z_ invites his partner to speak before him and listens as she speaks about how hard they had had to work in order to establish a successful business as immigrants to this country. D_ goes into detail about the sheer range of challenges that they have had to confront in order to get their legal status sorted out, as individuals and as a business entity. And if they had done all of this to attain their own legality, why would they want to risk it all for immigrants who could not be bothered to do that groundwork themselves? She doesn't have sympathy for people who wanted an easy out, D_ says. If people want to come to this country, they have to do it the right way. So no, she would not want to sponsor illegal immigrants. Those people should have come in legally. Like them.

Pause.

Taking his cue off her pause, Z_ contradicts his spouse. Speaking of the need for solidarity among immigrants, he says that he would be delighted to do his part in supporting people who have had to come into this country only to experience—for many of them—exactly the kind of repression that they were trying to flee. While he does agree with D_, in theory, that people should try to come into the country legally, Z_ engages his wife in a discussion about the various reasons why legality is a limited lens through which to view the validity of a person's arrival to a particular place.

Z_ looks at his S_ and putting her on the spot, asks about S_'s friend who had had first-hand experience of the immigrant detention system. Z_ and D_ had heard about this friend through their daughters' school's rumour mill. Mumbling, "Oh, I'm not . . . I'm just observi— can I use the restroom, actually?" S_ runs out of the room.

Pause.

A_ I think she's just . . . you know it's all really fresh and new. That's—ummm—yeah . . . like—Mom's friend was not able

to find another way to get into the country, you know . . . like, especially with the laws changing every day and everything . . .
I . . .
When did this country begin to become home for you? Is there . . . like . . . is there a particular thing that happened that made you realize that this is where you would build a life?

Silence.

Z_ and D_ look at each other, and it is clear that this is a difficult question for them to tackle. Not because they haven't thought about it before. Not because they have different opinions about the subject. Simply because they don't know. They go back and forth about it all the time.

On some days, this country does feel like home to them, and they know that the kind of life that they have here is not one that they could have if they lived in the country in which they had been born. On other days, though, all it would take is one comment, one glance, one change in policy, to make them realize that this place could never *really* be their home. That they will never be seen as *really* being from this land no matter how hard they try. However much they altered their names or their accents to be more of the land, their in-the-blood turns of phrase and their learned-from-birth lilts of speech would eventually slip out. Haunting them. Like unwelcome but undeniable ghosts of another time and place. So, what can they say in answer to A_'s question? How can they describe a home that always was and never could be? Two homes. Two lands. Two places that both kept them at arm's length.

A_ How do you live with that, like, dual-ness? Duality? Isn't it . . . difficult?

The couple can't help but smile at the simplicity of A_'s words. Difficult. Sure, it is difficult. It is difficult to carry duality with them, in them, through them. It is difficult to be from here and from there and not from here and not from there. It is difficult to feel at home in so many worlds and homeless in others. It is difficult. Absolutely. But the thing that makes it bearable, they say, are those fleeting moments of cohesion. Those brief wisps of time that happen occasionally, but not ever often enough, when it seems like there is something beyond here and there. When it feels like their homes across oceans and continents can actually coexist in an amorphous consciousness that only they can sense. Ephemeral notions of twin existences that can take their breath away, even after all these years, because they allow Z_ and D_ to feel a sense of belonging that surpasses national identity and geographical location. Brief explosions of liminality that make the everyday liveable. It is these bursts of coalescence, however infinitesimal, that shape the core of these immigrants' lives in this country. It is these moments that they live for; the moments in which everything comes together. Just like that.

A_ What do you miss the most? About that home?

What she misses the most, D_ says, is being there for her people. For the weddings. The birthdays. The heartbreaks. The spontaneous gatherings. The communal lamentations. D_ speaks about the funerals that she hasn't been there for. Like the funeral of her grandfather who died while she was in the middle of a multi-year process of getting her residential permit. D_ speaks about the goodbyes that she can never again say to a man she adores, even though she had said her farewell when she last saw him in person. That is what stings the most, D_ says. That when you leave a place and its people behind, you become more aware than ever that every goodbye could be the last one. And while that might be true of every person in every reality—that every goodbye might be the last one—there is a certain poignancy; a certain intensity; a certain heaviness in the air when you are leaving people across masses of land and water and memories and regret, with nothing more than the nebulous hope of a reunion in a year or more down the road. A lot can happen in a year.

D_ begins to sob uncontrollably. It is almost like the mention of her grandfather's funeral has unlocked all of the griefs that she has not yet grieved. Like the one from not being able to meet her sister's newborn child. Like the grief from not being able to attend her cousin's wedding. Not being able to be by her father's side when he was rushed into surgery. Not being able to hold her mother's hand as she was being medically quarantined. Not being able to sit in silence with her grandmother as they both looked at the chair her grandfather had always sat on. Not being able to be part of the pain of those who had, intentionally or not, consciously or not, willingly or not, allowed her to have the kind of life that she has on her good days in this country. Through heaving, unapologetic sobs, D_ speaks of everything that she misses about that home.

When moments like this happen, when an interviewee who is being spoken with as part of research shares their life in such an honest and vulnerable and visceral and gut-wrenching and unapologetic way, everything changes. Research becomes responsibility. Questions become intimacies. Answers become revelations. When a stranger discloses their scars because it is the only way in which they know how to bridge the gap between their life and that of the other before them, there is a burden that the listener takes on. A burden of witnessing that the listener has no choice but to take on.

When earthshattering truths are spoken in a language that isn't understood—like an immigration officer interviewing an asylum seeker who is speaking in their third language—it is easier for the listening officer to shape-shift, to evade, to distance, to evaluate.

When nerve-wracking vulnerabilities are shrouded and veiled in minimal sentences—like a mother trying to hide her scars from her daughter—it is easy for the observer to ignore the immensity of what it means to witness the demons of another. It is possible to think, one degree removed that—maybe—listening is the same as witnessing. That knowing could mean understanding. That awareness might imply doing.

When someone like D_ rips apart the façade, a listener's burden cannot go unacknowledged. Listening alone is not witnessing. Knowing alone does not mean understanding. Awareness alone does not imply doing.

S_ Are you OK, darling?
A_ Yeah. I'm OK. Just . . . you know.
Are you OK?

6 Safar

Part two

"Time for breakfast"

The Witness could decide to observe a murderer-turned-Detainee who is being given a tray of food—a dietitian approved combination of nutrients. They could continue observing as this Detainee chews their food, swallows their food, observes their food.

The Witness could decide to observe the mother-turned-Detainee who is in solitary confinement. She is being brought her food. She is staring at the food. Analyzing the food. Forcing down the food. Forcing out the food. Using the food and her bodily expulsions of it to make a protest mural on the walls of her cell.

The Witness could decide to observe the panopticon-esque architecture with its fluorescent lighting, its monochromatic walls and floors and ceilings and furniture and clothes, its bleach that covers the cafeteria tables, its cameras that are observing them (the Witness) observe the Officers observe the Detained, its cameras that are observing them observe the Detained who are observing the Officers, its cameras that are observing the Watchers and the Watched with an indiscriminate gaze.

The Witness could decide to observe the Officer who beats his spouse who is sitting down to eat with the Detainees. Who is refusing to eat the facility's food. Who is choosing to eat something they have brought from home, made by the person that he beats. Who is shooting the shit with the kitchen staff. Who is yelling at the Detainees for not eating their food in a prescribed way. Who is sitting down and staring into space, looking as if he is as much in detention as the Detained.

The Witness could decide to observe a fellow Witness. A young, passionate advocate for a particular manifestation of justice who is watching the Detained and their Detainers for any sign of unfair treatment. A budding activist like A_ who is watching the scenes that take

DOI: 10.4324/9781032685823-8

place before them with their own particular bias. An up-and-coming organizer who believes that the goal of dismantling the system should shape their entire existence.

-f-f-f-f-f-f-f-f-f-f-f-f-f-

"Time to finish breakfast"

The Witness can focus on the monotony of the fluorescent lighting and the monochromatic tones and the bleach and the cameras.

The Witness can focus on the Officer like S_ who does things because she finds herself in a situation where there doesn't seem to be any other option. Who feels boxed in. Who became an Officer because it is a role that has been passed down intergenerationally in her family. Who has gone down a path that she is unsure she should have ventured down. A path that she now finds herself on, regardless of what she might have wanted at a time long forgotten.

The Witness can focus on the mechanical responses of the Detainees who stop eating when they are told to. The Detainees who take their trays to a designated location when they are told to. The Detainees who dispose of their leftover food when they are told to. The Detainees who line up when they are told to. The Officers who ask the Detainees to line up when they are told to. The Officers who pat down the Detainees when they are told to. The Officers who lead the Detainees out when they are told to.

-f-f-f-f-f-f-f-f-f-f-f-f-f-

"COUNT"

The Detainees are counted by the Officers with support from the cameras.

One

Two

Three

Four

. . .

. . .

. . .

. . .

Until the registered number of Detainees is confirmed as present and accounted for.

This can take a while.

-f-f-f-f-f-f-f-f-f-f-f-f-f-

7 F for fences

Chikster,

My last breakfast at home for the foreseeable future and this is what I made. I think I've finally found the right way to interpret Achamma's instructions. Next time I make this, I'm probably—hopefully, most likely—going to be on your side of the world. And who knows, maybe you'll be making this for me. Or I'll be making this for you.

Idlis

- one measure idli rice
- quarter measure split urad dal
- one and a half measure thick aval/poha
- soak all of the above for four to five hours
- grind into the idli dough; the dough should look puffy and light, so don't add too much water while grinding; add salt just before you make idlis

Onion Sambar

Thoran dhal for half tin (three people)

- boil in pressure cooker (after sound for three minutes) with one and a half or two tumblers water
- mash well

Fry small onions little in oil and put in dhal

- boil with one glass of water nicely till onions are soft

DOI: 10.4324/9781032685823-9

Grind together and add after onions cook

- two fried tomatoes, cut in small pieces
- half tsp manya powder
- one tsp salt
- one small piece kayyam (quarter inch length)
- quarter tsp ulluva (fenugreek)
- some curry leaves
- two tablespoon kothamali
- four red chillies
- put one tbsp coconut oil. When hot, add kaduku, and when the seeds crackle, add one red chilli and karivapela (three leaves)
- remove from fire and pour the sambar into the oil
- pacha kothamali: add last before serving

The visa interview went much more easily than I thought. I was one of the lucky ones, though. A young girl in front of me was applying for a student visa. They asked her two questions—maybe even one—she was only up at the counter for like a minute. Before I knew it, they had rejected the visa, and she started sobbing as the official asked her to please leave the building.

There's this thing they've started doing, where if they give you the visa, they'll ask you to go to another counter down the end of the hall to pay the fee—don't know if that's how they did it in your day as well? That's how you know your application has been approved, how everyone in the room knows your application has been approved. The officer will give you your passport back and gesture to the end of the hallway.

The denial is equally visible. The officer will take this wooden stamp thing, that has DENIED or something like that on it. They slam it onto an ink pad and then stamp your passport. DENIED. As soon as the room sees the wooden thing being picked up, everyone knows. That poor fucker has just had their plans destroyed.

I was one of the lucky ones. The lawyer did a fantastic job with my application. The paperwork must have been excellent. I was worried that the officials would ask questions about my lack of employment and property and marriage. Or that they'd ask me for personal information about these friends who'd sent me these invitation letters when all I had was the most basic information about them. But the officer didn't ask me for any of that. She just looked at the paperwork and asked: "Which cities do you plan to visit?" And as soon as I answered that question, I was approved. It was that simple.

I went to see the family last week. It was tough. Really tough. Achamma is close to 90 now. They don't know the details. I just told them that I'm using this trip to see if I can find better opportunities there. That it's a more open culture. That it will be easier for me to live openly there. Of course, they understand that. I fear that if I tell them about the asylum plan, it will be too hard. Every day we hear in the news about how the government there is treating asylum seekers. Is it true that they're even separating children from their parents now? Hearing all of this on the news has them worried about my coming there even for a visit. So imagine if I told them the truth. They're immediately going to imagine me ending up a detention centre and getting tortured and killed or something. It's not that bad on the ground, is it?

It's strange. As I went through all this paperwork and bureaucracy, all I could think of was how lucky I am. How lucky that I have a network that was able to find a lawyer to advise me, free of cost. Imagine that. How lucky that I could afford the visa fees. That I could understand the forms. That I could fill them out in English. That I live close enough to the Embassy to not have to worry about getting there and spending money on hotels and transport. Through all the shit of the last few months, I still know I have had it so much easier than so many. I cannot even begin to imagine what it must be like to be on the run, in fear for your life, without having any of this kind of support at your disposal.

How are asylum seekers from those countries surviving through all of these nightmarish policies? I suppose that's what happens with shared borders. Neighbouring borders. Lord knows that anyone seeking asylum here, from one of our neighbouring countries, is likely to have a much tougher time that someone who comes from further away. What irony. All our lives we are told that we need to be good to the ones who live closest to us. After all, our neighbours are the ones who are closest when things go awry. They are the ones who are nearest when it's time for an impromptu celebration or an unexpected mourning. It's our neighbours that we share our fences with, our plot lines with, our leftovers with. It makes no sense to me why we are more inviting to people who come from opposite ends of the world, than we are to those come from just over there.

I remember thinking about it that year when I travelled to the fringes of this country. Lands that are shaped by a shared border with territories that are not here. Lands that are contained by arbitrary lines that separate us from peoples and cultures that we perhaps share more similarities with. Bordered lands. Borderlands . . . I read a beautiful book with that name recently and cannot help but think of my own body as being a borderland. A land between what I am and what I am expected to be. An in-between space that transgresses what is considered acceptable. A no-woman's land between what is desired and what is allowed. A vessel of unattained hopes and ravaged dreams. A land between borders. A border between lands.

It's the thought of the detention centres that I find most terrifying. The lawyer says that I might have to spend a few days—at the very least—at a detention centre, after I officially declare my intent to apply for asylum. It's less likely since I have a visa and can legally enter the country.

What if I'm arrested? The lawyer says it's not likely because I have legal representation and all of that, but detention is still on the table, as a possibility.

What if the lawyer gets hit by a car before she has a chance to file my papers? What will I do if something happens that makes her no longer able to represent me? What if she fucks up somehow and files the wrong papers or forgets to file something? What if I land up in one of those jails and no knows where I am, and I just get lost in the system? What if none of that happens but that they immediately put me on a plane home, and these goondas find me when I return and throw acid on me? What if this what if that what if then what if how what if nothing what if everything what if.

I feel like I'm losing my mind.

The panic attacks are getting worse. They used to happen a few times a week. Now it's like I live in a panic attack. Increased heart rate and sweaty palms and feeling the real is unreal and the unreal is real. Feeling like this time might be the time that I do not have control over my bladder and that I might pee my pants. Wondering if the people I am sitting with can see my mind racing at a million miles an hour, or if their bodies are deceiving them in the same way that mine is.

The only thing that helps right now is the thing that's always helped: cooking. It forces me outside the panic, and for whatever reason, while I remain petrified about peeing myself, I'm not afraid about having an accident with a knife or spluttering oil.

So I've been cooking, and saving it all for my friends to consume when I'm on my way.

After everything that has happened, each of them has a plan of their own. One of them is planning to seek asylum in a different country. One is planning to go back to their home town because he has high-powered relatives in a village in the middle of nowhere. One has decided to get married to throw them off the scent. Each of us is on our own path of persecution.

Whoever thought it would come to this.

When we were cooking in our dorms and eating maska buns and smoking cigarettes, I would never have thought in my wildest dreams that I'd be here.

A part of me is still hoping that, miraculously, by the time my asylum application is filed, officials here will have caught the motherfuckers who are after us, decide to disregard their influential families, and make a statement about protecting lives of people like me. Like us?

Even as I write that I realize how ludicrous that desire sounds. The only thing I can hope for is that with time, they—the fuckers who've made me resort to this—will have moved on. That they will have forgotten about us and this vendetta. That they will have found new obsessions to chase. And then, I will be able to come home again. To *my* country. A place where I find solidarity with my kind of people.

Maybe, by the time I apply for asylum, I won't need it anymore and can just come home.

That's a maybe I can get behind . . . But since I'm preparing for outcomes that I don't know to predict, if this might be the last time that you hear from me for who knows how long, there are some things that need to be said.

Thank you.

For being the first.

For opening my eyes to who I really am.

For breaking me so that I could learn how to put myself back together.

For putting me in a position to explore the nooks and crannies of the country that I will always call home, wherever I go, whatever I do. The place that I always took for granted. The place that I never have since that heartbroken expedition. That year. Thank you for making me question what I am willing to hide from the world, and what I am willing to share with it. For re-entering my life in the most unexpected of ways, and for giving me another reason to adore everything that food brings to my life. For always being a presence. In everything I've done. In everything I will do.

Clichés, perhaps. But times like these are made for clichés. Clichés are made for times like these. Right?

If things go as they should, if I am allowed into the country without a hitch and find my way to where I'm supposed to stay, I'll be in touch.

F_

8 Interview three

A_ So, what did you do?

P_ tells her about the first time she realized that she wanted to work with people who did not have a place to call home. P_ had visited a camp for displaced people in graduate school and recounts to A_ how she had sat with a group of displaced people under a tree, listening to their concerns, when she suddenly felt the need to take a shit. Not an it would be nice to take a shit situation, but an I'm going to soil my pants if I don't find a loo right now kind of situation. P_ describes in detail, with an occasional glance for approval at S_, the state of the toilet in that displaced people's camp: a building with different rooms that had no doors. No drainage. No plumbing. No toilet paper. No lights. No windows. A darkened concrete space that had what toilets contain. Piss. Shit. Blood. All in varying stages of decomposition. P_ explains the smell. The way the smell made the hairs on her arms stand up with their pungency. The way P_ had to tear pages out of her notebook—the one she was using to take notes for her research—in order to wipe her arse. This experience of defecation was seminal, P_ shares, in her decision to pursue a life in law. Law that focuses on displaced peoples. Peoples who are on the run from the places in which they were born. Peoples who find themselves looking for a new home. No one should have to shit in a place like that.

A_ Thank you so much, again, for taking the time to speak with me, and for, like, allowing my mother to sit in. Like I mentioned yesterday, I've learned so much through my internship here, and after what happened with my mother's, like . . . he—our family friend, she wanted to be here to listen to your responses.

DOI: 10.4324/9781032685823-10

So you've had students from my school volunteer here before, so you already know that we have students from very, like, powerful and, and, like, prominent immigrant families. One of the reasons I took this internship is because I also . . . you know, like . . . . want to find a way to get the families of our classmates to somehow help . . . I'm still figuring out, you know, like, exactly what it would mean to help. I mean, I have some thoughts, but I wanted to ask you, because of all your extensive experience, what you think . . . like . . . what young people our age can do to help the immigrants who are being held in detention centres.

P_ has seen many volunteers come through her offices in the last year, asking about ways they could help, asking for ways they could engage. And in one way, she loves answering questions about how to intervene and assist and demonstrate allyship. It comforts P_ that people are paying attention, especially when young people care. Whenever she loses faith in the system and the law, it is the well-intentioned volunteers who allow P_ to have hope that maybe things could be different tomorrow. But even through the slivers of hope that they provide, often, it feels to P_ like there are just too many of them. So many well-intentioned, naïve, ill-informed, big-hearted volunteers that P_, often, finds herself detesting the question—"What can I do to help?"—and its asker. Sometimes it feels to P_ like she spends so much time talking to volunteers like A_ about how they *might* help immigrants that she loses time from using the law to *actually* help.

Today, on the day that this young and bright-eyed legal intern decides to ask her the question, P_ is tired. She wants to get back to her clients; she wants to get back to amassing paperwork. But P_ forces herself to be generous and gracious. She knows that for young people like A_, approaching her is likely their initial foray into the minefield of thinking about others. And if that was the case, P_ has the power to shape how this young volunteer might grow and evolve into a fiery advocate for causes that she believes in. If that isn't reason enough, P_ thinks she sees a glimmer of desperation in the S_'s eyes. Like this mother needs to hear the answer to her daughter's question about how to support asylum seekers as much as or maybe even more than A_ does. An emanating anxiety that is not uncommon among those who have lost friends and family to a cavernous immigration detention complex.

A_ One of the things I've been wondering about . . . what is . . . something that might be done . . . I've been researching different

> concepts of, like . . . the differences between being a witness, versus a bystander, versus an observer, versus an ally . . . One of the ideas I've been thinking about is . . . what if . . . like . . . I know it may sound silly but . . . what if officers at detention centres were given jobs at other places so that those of them who disagree with the government policy on detention can . . . like . . . can have a way to leave without worrying about their jobs? You know? I don't know if that makes sense, but I . . . like . . . I know offering jobs to detention centre officers might be a really strange idea, but I was just thinking about what could be . . . like . . . a creative solution and I don't know . . . this idea just like . . . came to mind . . . especially if these jobs were offered by, like, immigrant families like the ones in our school . . . you know? Where people like . . . like my family . . . what if every family like ours creates jobs for people within the system who would lose their jobs if they protested unfair and unjust laws? How many of those, like . . . how many of those questioning officials would leave . . . and then . . . yeah, does that even make sense?

Rarely does she come across a concept that she honestly has never thought of before. For years now, all of P_'s focus has been on immigrants' and asylum seekers' plight in a constantly changing landscape of policy and action. For the last year, in particular, all of her focus had been on finding ways to get detained immigrants and asylum seekers out on bond or parole and on finding ways for her clients to locate sponsors who would host them till their day in court. In being so solely focused on her client base, she hasn't really thought about the officers or about how the carceral system might be dismantled from the inside. P_ has always thought that state officials are less worthy of her attention because of their role in perpetuating and manifesting an unjust system; A_'s idea is not going to change her mind on that front. However, whatever her personal disdain for the officers might be, and however strong her instinctual response that even creative ideas like A_'s can't make more than a slight dent in the abolition of a neocolonial prison industrial complex, P_ is impressed at the ingenuity of what A_ is describing to her.

The approach that the A_ is sharing with her is not one that is within P_'s wheelhouse. In fact, A_'s idea is completely outside P_'s frame of reference. So, what can she offer as a response in this moment? How can the more experienced advocate advise the young volunteer when no one could have the faintest idea how an initiative like the one A_ is proposing would work in reality? A_'s is a new idea. An experimental idea. And like all new and experimental ideas, the only option would be to take a risk. Risk. Fail. Risk again. Fail again. Fail differently. That's all there is to do when a new idea needs to be tested, right? And that's all P_ can tell her A_: "Try your idea. See what happens."

S_ Can I —

A_ Of course, Amma.

S_ Thank you for allowing me to be here. A_ has said so many wonderful things about you, and now I understand why . . . So I'm like A_'s assistant on this project, and it's not my role to ask questions but, you know, sh—he—m—our family friend—tried to seek asylum here and after everything that happened, I wanted to ask just one thing: what will change the situation? On a larger, societal level, what will need to happen for the government to reconsider some of these policies?

P_ responds with a disclaimer that her response to this question is geared toward people like her. Citizens. Members of a privileged socio-economic class. People from a racial or ethnic group that has less reason to fear state violence. Individuals who hold some or many forms of these relative advantages. P_ talks about the need for these relatively privileged bodies to come forward. Bodies that are less likely to need to fear life or death consequence. It's bodies that need to stand outside every single immigrant detention centre in every single part of the country, P_ says. These bodies need to station themselves outside any and all manifestations of the state that contain immigrants and asylum seekers and, once there, once these bodies are stationed on the perimeters of such locations, they have to be ready and willing to put their lives on the line. They, the inhabitants of these privileged identities, need to come together in such large numbers that the government will have no choice but to change its policies. There needs to be so many privileged bodies out there, on the streets, that offices close. Hospitals become inoperable. Schools lie vacant. There needs to be enough privileged bodies putting themselves on the line for enough time that there is a fracture to the backbone of this country's capitalist machine. Only then will things change, P_ says. Only then will be there be the remotest chance of things changing. When the government realizes that there could be dire consequences at home for the bodies that they imprison from overseas.

A_ So . . . one of the ways I am thinking about reaching people is creating a simulated journey of some kind—my da—w—I have connections to a company that creates those and types of—they're called Safars . . . I've been working with them on trying to think about . . . the kind of immersion that would give someone who has no experience of the immigration detention system . . . like . . . it can give them a more . . . like so that people here can put themselves in the shoes of those who are being detained . . . sorry if I'm being un—it's still a new idea and . . . like . . . I've just started drafting something, and once it's done, if you have time, I would love to get your feedback as well, but like . . . for this Safar or like, simulation . . . since you've spent so much time in the detention centres, what is one thing that happens there, inside the centres, that you think that people here should experience as part of this Safar that we're designing?

"Monotony." That's what P_ is always struck by when she goes into the detention centres. The absolute monotony under which the detainees—who are doctors, lawyers, miners, engineers, construction workers, professors, mothers, tailors, fathers, social workers, children, teachers, nurses, and some abusers, drug lords, psychopaths—are caged. A monotony within which the detained are told how to spend every waking minute. Every sleeping minute. Every shitting minute. A monotony which is punctuated by the detained being counted like sheep. Exploited as indentured labour. Isolated from each other for the smallest mishap. Watched as they eat. Watched as they sleep. Watched as they shit. Watched. Watched. Watched. As they live through a monotony that makes them waste away in visible and invisible ways.

There are other things too, of course, that P_ believes everyone should know about. The physical violations. The lack of healthcare. The missing mental health support. The abuses of power. The heart-wrenching separations. The bone-chilling architecture. The shit inducing fluorescent lights. The nauseating stench of bleach and every other kind of cleaning and sanitizing agent. The wails of the guilty and the guiltless; the victims and the perpetrators. There are many, many things that the outside world needs to know about those prison walls and what they perpetuate. But right now, in this moment, if P_ has to choose one thing above all else, it would have to be the monotony.

A_ I'm glad you felt comfortable enough to ask a question.
S_ Really? I didn't know if I would be interrupting you.
A_ No! I want these interviews to feel, like, a conversation, you know? It's nice to have you also be part of it. Really, whenever you feel like, feel free to chip in and ask a question or respond to something. That way you'll feel more like part of things.
S_ Thank you, baby.
A_ For what?
S_ For being open to this. To me. After everything.

9 Safar

Part three

"Liminal time"

The Witness may notice the Witness like ____ in their midst. The one who thrives in identifying the big ideas. The cross-genre connections. The anthropological patterns. The one who thinks that everything is relative. Truth. Justice. Morality. Even history. The one who believes that if everything is relative, solutions cannot exist; all that can exist are differing interpretations of the problem.

The Witness may notice the corrosive dynamics that are fostered by the fluorescent lighting, the monochromatic walls and floors and ceilings and furniture and clothes, the all-pervasive bleach, the cameras that are noticing how the Witness notice the Officers who are taking notice of the Detained.

The Witness may notice a librarian-turned-Detainee who is taking a shit, before sitting and staring, after meditating, before masturbating, all while sobbing.

The Witness may notice an Officer who detests their job but needs the money. This Officer watches the Detainees through the sliver of glass on their cell doors. Then this Officer behaves with one of the Detainees in a way that they absolutely should not. Then this Officer completes lots and lots of paperwork. Then this Officer watches a porno on their facility-sanctioned device. Then this Officer dons a particular look, making them seem like they are as much in detention as the Detained.

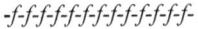

-f-f-f-f-f-f-f-f-f-f-f-f-f-

"Free time"

The Witness might elect to perceive the Detainees who are watching TV—a carefully curated selection of channels and shows that they

DOI: 10.4324/9781032685823-11

don't have too much of a say in. Or the Witness might elect to perceive the Detainees who are playing board games. Or the Detainees who are checking out a designated number of books from the library. Or the Detainees who doing their laundry, returning one dirty item for a clean one. Or the Detainees who are performing bodyweight exercises.

The Witness might elect to perceive the privileged among the Detainees who are getting more than one hour of supervised time on a computer. Or the privileged among the Detainees who are getting more than their one hour of time outdoors. Or the Detainees who are visiting the facility Counsellor because they are afflicted by one of the range of conditions that is likely to be induced/worsened by settings of detention and incarceration. Or the Witness might elect to perceive the mother-turned-Detainee who is still in solitary confinement. For this Detainee, all time is free time. All time is the same time.

Or the Witness might elect to perceive the Detainee who is like S_'s ex. Someone who, at one point or another—maybe at this point, maybe another—was deemed as being unstable. Mentally ill. Psychologically unwell. And due to a confluence of circumstances, this S_'s ex-husband-like Detainee now finds themselves in detention. Detained so that they don't harm themselves. Detained so that they don't harm others. Detained because the differences they embody have been deemed unfit in a society that has a particular definition of the fit.

The Witness might elect to perceive an addict Officer who is playing a boardgame with the Detained. Who then tries to break up a fight. Who then tries to deal with a family emergency, while at work, without being able to get time off because the facility is understaffed. Who then needs to visit the facility Counsellor because she is struggling with one of the many conditions that are more likely to be induced/worsened in/by settings of detention and incarceration. The addict Officer who is as much in detention as the Detained.

-f-f-f-f-f-f-f-f-f-f-f-f-f-

"Time to consult your lawyer"

The Witness can attempt to discern the complexities that arise as a child-turned-Detainee meets with a legal representative, without another adult on his side being present. As this child-turned-Detainee is met with ambiguous answers that do not seem to provide any sense of certainty, as this child-turned-Detainee is made to fill and refill forms that they can barely read, let alone understand, the Witness might see him tell his Lawyer that he couldn't meet the day before because his unit's Officer was in a bad mood. As the same Officer listens to the ongoing interactions between child-turned-Detainee and his lawyer. As the same Officer offers to translate between Detainee and lawyer because they happen to speak the language and today, the Office happens to be in a good mood.

The Witness can attempt to discern the complexities that arise when an Officer like ______ declares their passion for serving the state (or the corporate runners of the facility, who represent the state). This Officer might be like A_'s father. Articulate. Earnest. Smart. Passionate. Not the archetypal boor who goes around brandishing a baton, but a businessman who can articulate the precise need for the existence of someone like them and a facility like this.

The Witness can attempt to discern the complexities that arise when another Officer who is a single-parent deals with personal issues on his unsanctioned personal device. When this Officer loses his temper and takes out his rage on the room's vending machine. When this parent spends more time than necessary, it seems, in the restroom. When this parent-Officer emerges from the restroom only to taunt and chide the child-turned-Detainee his breath. Or loudly. Is this parent-Officer as much in detention as the child-turned-Detainee?

-f-f-f-f-f-f-f-f-f-f-f-f-f-

"COUNT"

The Detainees are counted by the Officers with support from the cameras.

One

Two

Three

Four

. . .

. . .

. . .

. . .

. . .

Until the registered number is confirmed as being present and accounted for.

This can take a while.

-f-f-f-f-f-f-f-f-f-f-f-f-f-

10 F for few and far between

Dear Chikaroni,

I'm here!

This city is big. HUGE. There is such an extensive system of flyovers and roads, and the speeds here are terrifying. People think it's normal to drive at 85 mph, and they have the gall to poke fun at *our* traffic? Please. This is NUTS. Why are they all in such a hurry?

I thought about calling you rather than writing, but you sounded a little off in your last message, and I didn't think it would be wise to call if something is not quite right at home.

I'm here, Chikster. I made it through that dreaded port of entry questioning. They didn't ask me very much. Why are you here? When are you leaving? Bang, bang, boom. Stamped. In the country.

The lawyer has me in a hostel type situation for now. It's not really a family that's hosting me, like I thought from the letter. Apparently, they made the letter sound like that so that it'd seem more legit for the tourist visa application. This place is an apartment complex type thing—run by a local group—that functions as a hostel for asylum seekers. They cover our housing and food costs. We chip in for the latter when we can.

They run this place like a community. A co-op, I think, is the better-known term? We all help with everything. Cooking, cleaning, laundry. I must admit that the shee-shee-me who has always had household help to do all of these things at home is having a little bit of a tough time adjusting. Specially to cleaning the toilet. I think the others here think I'm strange because I need instructions on how to do the most basic tasks. I haven't washed my clothes by hand in so long, da. I honestly don't think I'm doing much except moving my dirty clothes around in soapy water. Luckily there are others here to teach me. And my way of giving back has been to do some cooking, which luckily,

DOI: 10.4324/9781032685823-12

I have funds to go get groceries for (many of the folks here don't even have that). That and I've been spending time with anyone here, with kids mostly, who want to learn English. I'm not much of a teacher, but at least it's a way to pass the time, and to contribute in a more tangible manner than my sloppy cleaning efforts.

Of course, one of the highlights for me has been trying all this amazing food. I tried some circular bread with sugar topping in the shape of a conch the other day, and this amazing sauce with chocolate in it. S_, if I had known that there was such amazing cuisine here, I would have put you to work and had you sent me recipes too!

Most of the day is spent waiting for my lawyer to call. She calls me once a day to check in and gives me an update on what the latest is. The laws are changing every day, and every day it seems like she gives me a slightly different answer about when we should file my asylum papers. Before I got here, it sounded like we would file the papers the day after I arrived in the country. But now, the lawyer says that we should wait a bit so that it doesn't seem like I lied outright in my tourist visa interview. There's no clarity about what "a bit" is, though. There are some people who've been living in this co-op for two weeks. Others have been here for a few months. Each one's case seems to be slightly similar and slightly different. Similar enough for all of us to think of asylum as being the only way for us to live our futures with some semblance of safety. Different enough where all our lawyers tell us slightly different things about when we need to file our applications and what exactly we should expect after that. It all seems so random. Some of the people here came here with no papers and somehow, didn't get sent to a detention centre. Others came with papers but had to spend time in a facility of some kind. Some were separated from their children. Others were let through with their kids. No one knows why their application seems to have been dealt with in a particular way. It seems like the decisions are often arbitrary and depend on a range of intersecting factors. So, sometimes, someone's immigration or asylum fate depends on the officer that they speak to at the particular point of entry through which they happen to be entering the country—that immigration officer's personal and political beliefs; their approach to following orders; hell, it sometimes seems to simply depend on a border officer's mood in a given moment. It seems like the decisions that are meted out can also shift based on the legal advice that people entering the country receive. On whether the person entering the country has a lawyer or not. Whether they have a family or not.

On which particular section of a border they enter through. The decisions can also vary, apparently, based on the directives that have been issued on a particular day around the time that a particular person tries to cross a particular section of the border. It all seems so haphazard, in a way that I didn't expect.

Having grown up listening to such glorified stories about this country, I guess I always thought that they had shit figured out much better than we did. That somehow their bureaucrats would be more efficient. That their government representatives would be more organized. That their laws would make more sense. But turns out, this place is as much of a shit show as home. This shit show just has central air conditioning and a seemingly never-ending supply of hot water. Now, *that* I won't complain about. The high-pressure showers with so much hot water! I think I took like five showers on my first day here, till someone told me that we were living in a desert and that we should be trying to limit our use of water. Now I just shower once a day. Twice if no one's looking.

I have a room to myself. It's a small space. Just enough to fit a bed and a desk and a window and a wash basin. I've also taken up meditation to pass the time. Wouldn't my folks be proud? All those years they tried to get me into yoga and meditation, and I kept resisting. And here, in this foreign land, I'm trying to channel everything I've heard about meditation over the years, to see if it will become a way for me to pass the time more quickly.

Why did you sound so off in your last message, C.? Everything's OK, I hope? I thought you would be all rejuvenated after your family vacation. I asked people here and apparently you were vacationing not that far from where I am now. I completely understand why you would choose to holiday in a place near this one. It is beautiful here. And if it were not for the nightmares and the anxiety and the still incessant panic attacks, I might be able to convince myself that I'm here on some kind of a holiday, you know? It's just hard to keep any kind of positivity when things are the way they are.

The other day, all of us who are staying at the co-op were preparing one of our communal meals—there are about twenty of us here now, who'll likely be here for a while—when another group came through just for the day. They were just passing through. This happens often. A new group of people arrives, they take a shower, have a meal, and then take off in unmarked vehicles. It's all very ominous. A few of us were cooking the other day when one such group came in. One of the people in the long-term crew (which is what we call ourselves now), who is a musician, had brought out this box-like thing that he used as a drum. Anyway, we were all singing and talking, and for a while, for a few precious hours, it felt almost like we were just a group of people hanging out and enjoying a lovely evening with friends. And then one of those ominous vans came in. A van that, on that day, happened to be loaded with children. Two adults and ten kids, ranging in ages from two to sixteen. It was obvious that the kids were not all biologically related to the adults. Actually, I don't think any of the kids were biologically related to the adults. I'm still a little bit unclear as to who the adults were in relation to the children. Whatever the case, the vehicles pulled in, and the kids poured out of the van one after the other: dishevelled, sad, and carrying a weight that no one their age should even know exists. I couldn't understand the specifics of what was being discussed (we always use such a mishmash of languages that everyone needs to be content understanding a tenth of what is going on). But despite the language barriers and the cultural barriers and all the other kinds of barriers, what was clear was that the kids were not with their families. That they were dislocated. Disenfranchised. Is that even the right word? The music had to change its tone then. It was still there, the music. The music is always there. It doesn't ever go away. But it changes. It shifts. Its rhythms and melodies become suffused with the guts of the air. And when the air has entrails that are formed by the cries of children, one must ask, what is music anymore?

There's one nightmare that keeps coming back to me. An ominously white substance flies, and as it does, the sun glistens through its bubbles and the light fissures through its fumes. And in that moment, as the viscosity of the material and the texture of its flow create a delicate pattern in the air, this winged amalgamation of fluid and gas and permeable solid exudes a heat that its intended recipient will feel on their skin a few seconds later. A heat that will be accompanied by a pungent stench that singes hair and eats through flesh, maybe even bone. A quick and prolonged suffocation. A flash of texture and smell and temperature and weight that will become almost breathtaking in its magnificence. Till it lands on the person it is being aimed at. Till it lands on the person it is aimed at and sears through their flesh. Till it lands on the person it is aimed at, sears through their flesh, and leaves behind scars that will bizarrely mirror the earthen elements that it propels through to find its landing strip. The human body rather than the air. The body that it will mark with imprints that bubble and froth and fume and exhale and bubble and blister and explode in tiny crackles, till the carrier of those scars is blinded by a pain that can draw them out of even the deepest of slumbers into the grasp of a reality that will never seem to release its grip. The smell. Burning flesh. Pustules that will form because of the heat. Translucent globules that will seem like they are filled with water, making their wearer want to score them with a blade to see what might lie beneath. Watery boils that will be contrasted in their colour and texture with the black and purple hues of a skin that has never felt or looked or smelled or tasted or sounded less like skin. Boils and blisters and scars and ruptures that will ooze and bleed and puss and smell that will exude a heat that seems to burn from the outside in. Or the inside out. An oozing and bleeding and puss-ing and smelling that will locate its meeting point somewhere in borderlands between the outside-in and the inside-out and that will climax in a white-hot explosion that is so painful that it can be seen and heard and smelled and tasted.

Every night, it's the same images. The same wake up call. The same smells and sounds and visions that refuse to let me rest.

I ache for home.

F_

11 Interview four

I_ has agreed to meet with A_ and S_ because his current job as a mall guard is monotonous, and he needs a diversion. This former correctional officer is sure that he knows what A_ is thinking when she came to interview him. He thinks he knows because he has heard it all before, of course. All these people who looked at him and see his skin colour and hear his accent and think that there is no way in which an immigrant like him could support the criminal justice system.

I_ has never understood that logic. So he had not been born in this country. So he had sought refuge here. So, what? What did any of that have to do with his having been a correctional officer? That's what he had done in the land of his birth too. That's what he had been raised to do in the country that he had fled from. It only seemed to make sense, then, that that's what he would want to do in his new home, to pay back the country that had taken him in as one of their own.

I_ hates it when bleeding hearts in this country look askance at him for having been part of the prison system. He is sick of hearing their arguments and their propaganda and their bullshit. But still. He has a soft spot for young people, I_ does. He likes telling them about his life and opening their minds to new ideas. They can become officers too, if they only apply themselves to the task.

A_ What are the similarities between being a correctional officer here and having the same position in your country?

I_ first clarifies for A_ that *this* is his country. But yes, he can tell her about the similarities between being an officer of the law in this country and the place in which he happened to have been born. He tells her how this country is so much more efficient than the country

DOI: 10.4324/9781032685823-13

in which he had been initially trained. How this country is so much better at anticipating who is more likely to commit crimes and at preventing more serious future crimes by incarcerating based on predictabilities rather than current fact. The key to this country's justice system, I_ says, is that the government of this nation has figured out which demographic is more likely to commit crimes than another. This government has, over decades, and perhaps even centuries of incisive strategic thinking, manifested complex codes of conduct and legality that have ensured that the kinds of citizens who are more likely to commit crimes than others are more likely to find their way into the prison system at an early age. How fantastic. The land of his birth has not been quite so efficacious, I_ says, and the legal system there takes years to ensure justice. The government in his birthplace actually tries *not* to incarcerate people, using considerable tax-payer resources in order to rehabilitate. Rehabilitate. "As if that's even possible," I_ says. That government has never accepted the fact that some people are just genetically more predisposed to committing crimes than others. I_ says that he loves how this country believes the opposite.

A_ I see. So you think that the criminal justice system here works and that other countries need to learn from . . . I . . . Sorry, that wasn't what I was . . . so let me just . . . sorry, that just . . . caught me off . . . the information I've come across is that correctional officers are more likely to become alcoholics, or addicts, or have dysfunctional home lives . . . and that, you know, that, like, prisons have as much of a negative effect on the officers, as they do on the detained.

I_ shares, in no uncertain terms, that he does not agree with A_'s research. Weak-willed officers are few and far between, he says, and are the ones who are not strong enough to take on the job. It's the officers who are not disciplined enough to control their urges who struggle; I_ believes that his own past has made him tough. Strong. Better able and more adept when it came to handling life in prison than his peers who had lived privileged lives and didn't quite understand the need for well-orchestrated spaces of discipline and punishment. I_ thinks that it is this type of softness in the face of crime that has led to people like him having to flee their homeland. Unfortunately for I_, in the country of his birth, he had become a correctional officer during a year in which a new government had come into power. A new government which deemed officers like him to be "too aggressive." Fuck them.

It was I_'s views about the importance of law enforcement that had made him a refugee to begin with. And only this nation, his new home, had immediately identified his promise and given him a new context in which to nurture his values and beliefs. The research that A_ is referencing, I_ thinks, is based on the narratives of fragile officers who join the system with no conviction in the greater good that they are serving by being part of it. These motherfuckers join the forces for all the wrong reasons. That's why they complain and drink and abuse substances. It is their own fault if they feel imprisoned by the prisons in which they work. Not the prisons. "You need to find new research."

A_ I see . . . Thank you for being so . . . like . . . direct in sharing your thoughts with me.
Given your experience with the criminal justice system in this country, what do you think about this new trend that has come up about asylum seekers and immigrants being separated from their families and being put into detention centres?

For the first time in their chat, I_ is quiet. And when he speaks, his response surprises A_. From everything that he has said until this point, A_ thinks she can predict I_'s response to her question. That he will reveal himself to be an avid supporter of the separations and the detentions. After all, isn't the government framing the entire immigration conversation as one about outsiders being more likely to commit crimes than citizens of their own country? And if I_ approves of the proclivity of the leaders in this country to cage *potential* criminals as much as *actual* criminals, as he has said, wouldn't he strongly approve of the toughest of policies to punish the law breakers?

To A_'s surprise, though, this is one area where I_ doesn't think that the law is in the right. He seems genuinely conflicted between his absolute belief in the legal system of this country, and its enactment in this particular regard. He can't understand it, I_ tells A_, because when he first heard the government's arguments for the separations and for the detention of immigrants and asylum seekers, they made sense to him. I_ initially saw reason in the government's framing of the situation as a law-and-order issue. And yet, when I_ thought about families being ripped apart and children being held in cages, even this former correctional officer had to admit the egregiousness of this manifestation of the law.

I_ knows that his response isn't entirely logical. He knows that his disagreement with this governmental action might stem from looking at images and faces and seeing reflections of himself and his children. I_ knows that the dis-ease that he is feeling likely comes from the particular labels that he happens to share with the people who are languishing behind these prison bars—immigrants. Asylum Seeker. Father. Husband. I_ realizes that that his scepticism of this manifestation of the justice system, in the face of so many others, makes him a little bit of a hypocrite. And so, he knows to expect A_'s next question before she even needs to ask it: why the double standard?

I_ can't give A_ a better answer than simply saying that it is easier to sympathize with someone who shares aspects of his life experience than it is for him to identify with someone who has grown up in different circumstances. Perhaps it comes down to the simple fact, I_ says, that the immigrants and asylum seekers who come to this country are mostly fleeing oppressions and conditions that are unimaginable to the citizens of here. So, perhaps some degree of illegality is acceptable, given their desperation? As I_ sees it, most lawbreakers in this country don't have anything to be desperate about.

A_ But that isn't entirely true, right? I mean . . . maybe you're right on a more, like, general scale. That more people in this country have access to better starting points than people in the places from which some of the asylum seekers are escaping. But still, aren't there enough people here who are destroyed by their own forms of, like . . . desperation? So many people here who are suffering under the weight of centuries of systematic, like, oppression? Don't these people have as much of a right or need to battle the law when . . . like . . . the law continues to be the thing that supports their oppression? And—if you'd just let me finish—aren't there some asylum seekers and immigrants who, in their countries, might have had more access to resources than some people in this one?

I_ gives A_ a look. A look that is meant to convey his disapproval of her comments. A look that conveys his disdain at being spoken down to, patronized—as he sees it—by a girl who is young enough to be his granddaughter. A look that tells A_ that this former correctional officer doesn't really have much more to contribute to the conversation. I_ asks A_ about what she is going to do with all this information she is collecting. And when she tells him about the broad strokes of her idea for a Safar, I_ laughs. Mockingly. Patronizingly. Cruelly, and asks A_ if she really is arrogant enough to think that she is going to get anything done as a young high school student who has no personal knowledge about what it means to be either an asylum seeker or an correctional officer or anything, really. What does she think she can achieve? I_ laughs at A_. Derisively. Contemptuously.

S_ Look, sir, there's no need to speak to my daughter like that.

Even when his responses cause I_ to see something akin to a glimmer of tears in A_'s eyes, he cannot stop himself from further berating her ideals.

S_ Sir, please calm down. She's a teenager.

But I_ can't seem to do that. He can't stop himself from launching into an effusive tirade against how children like her didn't understand the struggles that their elders had to undergo in order to give them a comfortable life in this country.

S_ Please lower your voice.

I_ cannot stop his derisive comments even when a few tears escape down A_'s cheeks.

S_ Sir —

I_ cannot resist saying, as A_ cries quietly, that children need to know their place and wait and watch and learn until they are ready and experienced enough to challenge the complicated status quos that governed the world around them.

S_ HEY. STOP. DON'T YOU DARE SPEAK TO MY DAUGHTER THIS WAY.

He stops.

S_ You can be sure your supervisors will hear about this.

As they walk away, shaken, S_ drapes her arm around A_'s shoulders.

A_ Don't file a complaint. It's OK. I was pushing him.
S_ No, you weren't pushing him. You were presenting a different opinion than his, and he lost his temper.
Don't blame yourself for something that's not your fault, darling. Too many young women do that. Too many.

Silence.

A_ Thanks, Amma.
S_ For what?
A_ For standing up for me.

12 Safar

Part four

"Time for lunch"

The Witness could reflect on the long-term repercussions of living with constant fluorescent lighting/ of existing within intentionally un-individualized monochromatic walls and floors and ceilings and furniture and clothes/of inhaling the fumes of cleaning agents/ of always being recorded by cameras that are watching the Witness watching the Officers watching the Detained/ of Detainees who are being told what to eat, when to eat, how to eat/ of the Detainees who are being watched as they perform the seemingly mundane steps that are involved in the mastication and swallowing of food/ of Detainees who have to eat alone while in extended solitary confinement/ of Officers who never know when the next emergency might emerge/ of one kind of Officer, who engages respectfully with the Detained in the post-lunch pat-downs/ of another second kind of Officer, who does quite the opposite/ of yet a different third kind of Officer who seems apathetic/of all the kinds of Officers, who seem to be as much in detention as the Detained.

Perhaps this Witness, the one who is reflecting on long-term repercussions, is someone like S_. Someone who, at some point, didn't really care about all the things that were happening to people like the Detainees. Someone who, suddenly, finds a personal reason to care. Someone who, once that personal connection was ignited, finds that there is no turning back. Perhaps this Witness, who is like S_, cannot understand how apathetic their earlier self was. Isn't the political always personal? Shouldn't it be?

-f-f-f-f-f-f-f-f-f-f-f-f-f-

DOI: 10.4324/9781032685823-14

"Time to finish lunch"

The Witness may choose to reflect on systemic codes that programme everyone and everything to do what they are told do. When they are told to. For the most part. Even the Detainee like _____. Someone who is a thinker. Someone who used to be on the frontlines of scholarship in their country, only to one day find themselves being persecuted for having discovered or written about an idea that the powerful did not agree with. And just like that, over night, the scholar becomes an asylum seeker who has to flee. Like _____, this Detainee is also married to the love of their life. This Detainee, like _____, also has a child. This Detainee, unlike _____, has no idea where their spouse and child are being held. And so, does what they are told to. To increase the odds that they might see their own again.

-f-f-f-f-f-f-f-f-f-f-f-f-f-

"COUNT"

The Detained are counted.

By the Officers.

With support from the cameras.

One

Two

Three

Four

. . .

. . .

. . .

. . .

. . .

Until the registered number is confirmed as being present and accounted for.

This can take a while.

-f-f-f-f-f-f-f-f-f-f-f-f-f-

"Time for work"

The Witness might deign to look at the Detainees who are being asked to sew. Being told to sew. Being ordered to sew. The Detainees who are being asked to clean toilets. Being told to clean toilets. Being ordered to clean toilets. The Detainees who are being asked to garden. Being told to garden. Being ordered to garden. The Detainees who are being asked to cook. Being told to cook. Being ordered to—you get the point. The Detainees who are being told to launder. The Detainees who are being ordered to just sit in their cells. The cameras that don't discriminate. Unless their users tell them to. The Officers who are observing the Detained workers with scrutiny, making sure that they aren't pocketing tools that they shouldn't be. The Officer who is sitting quietly in the corner, with circles beneath her eyes. The Officer in another corner, with puffy eyelids. The Officers who are engaging in what seems to be flirtatious verbal foreplay. With each other. With an un-consent-able Detainee. The Witness might deign to look at the Officers who seem to be as much in detention as the Detained.

One of the Officers that the Witness is deigning to look at might be like F_ Someone who came to this country as a refugee, but who—unlike F_—was let in. And in an act of loyalty to the country that has opened its doors to them, this Officer defends the new country from others like the them that they used to be. Maybe this Officer sees the disconnect between who they were then and who they are now. Or maybe this Officer is so immersed in this new reality that, like F_, they feel an ache to give back to the land they call home. Unlike F_, maybe this Officer conflates the idea of a homeland with the construction of a nation-state. They don't see that serving one's country might have nothing to do with defending a government.

-f-f-f-f-f-f-f-f-f-f-f-f-f-

"Free time"

The Witness could just as well choose not to see or look at or pay attention to anything. They could choose to not to see or look or pay attention to the Detainee like ______. Someone who lost a brother at an early age. Someone who comes from a very rich family but lost it all because he pissed off the wrong person in power. Maybe this Detainee, like someone else finds themselves in the facility, waiting for their family to pull the strings to get them out. Maybe this ______-like Detainee finds themselves in the facility, knowing that it is only a matter of time before their connections work out the kinks. Maybe this is the elite Detainee. The one who knows that their time in prison is temporary. Time-bound. Unlike the others.

-f-f-f-f-f-f-f-f-f-f-f-f-f-

"Time for dinner"

The Witness could choose to ignore the Officer like ______. Idealistic. Passionate. More of a follower than a leader. Maybe the Officer took this job because they had a mentor who urged them to change the system from the inside. Maybe this Officer took this job to "be the change." To be an Officer who embodies kindness and respect toward the Detained that they watch over. Of course, what the Officer does not understand is that systems like these are not designed for exceptions.

-f-f-f-f-f-f-f-f-f-f-f-f-f-

"Time to finish dinner"

There might be a Witness who used to be idealistic. "What is the point of caring?" this Witness now wonders. "It's all going to shit anyway." Perhaps they show up to witness the Detained because of some warped sense of responsibility. Does showing up as a Witness mean anything, if the outcome of that witnessing is a foregone conclusion?

The Detainees still stop eating when they are told to.

The Detainees still take their tray to a designated location when they are told to.

The Detainees still consent to being patted down when they are told to.

An Officer hugs one of the Detainees, without being told to (they are immediately removed from the scene).

An Officer beats one of the Detainees, without being told to (they are immediately removed from the scene).

An Officer can remain cool and detached from the Detained, as they are told to (they are allowed to remain at the scene).

Everything is the same.

Till it isn't.

-f-f-f-f-f-f-f-f-f-f-f-f-f-

"COUNT"

The Detained are counted.
By the Officers.
With support from the cameras.
One
Two
Three

Four

. . .

. . .

. . .

. . .

. . .

Until the registered number is confirmed as being present and accounted for.

This can take a while.

-f-f-f-f-f-f-f-f-f-f-f-f-

"Lights out"

The Witness can't see anything anymore.

They can't see the Detainee whose fate might mirror F_'s. Someone who has found themselves in this facility despite their best laid plans. Someone who has recently had an epiphany about life being defined by how one deals with the choices one has made. Someone who has found solidarity in the sameness that they share with others among the Detained.

The Witness can't see anything anymore.

They can't see the Detainee who decides that they want to stand up for a newfound friend, a fellow prisoner, a mother-turned-Detainee. Who decides that they want to stage a protest in the facility, to support the release of that mother who has been separated from her child. Who spends all their lights-out-time designing and planning a protest.

The Witness can't see anything anymore.

They can't see the Detainee who decides to go on a hunger strike, to force the Officers to allow a mother to visit her sick child who is languishing in a detention centre somewhere (maybe even this one). Who, in the midst of the strike, collapses. Who, post-collapse, does not get the medical attention that is needed. Who might never again see the world that lies outside prison walls.

The Witness can't see anything anymore.

Even if they want to.

-f-f-f-f-f-f-f-f-f-f-f-f-

13 F for (so close and yet so) far

We've been passing time by doing mock interviews. One of us pretends to be the immigration officer, and the other person, as themselves, must answer the fake officer's questions. Apparently, during the real interview, the officers ask the same questions that are already on the application form but want even more detail. I'm told that it's good practice, for us to get used to talking about things that we'd rather not rehash, and to get better at recounting things that we don't want to mention, let alone describe or explain. It's also good practice, I guess, for us to speak with someone whose accent or even language we don't understand. Good practice that feels like a dystopic role-playing exercise.

In the last week, we've had a group of women come through the co-op. Women who are fleeing from gangs. Women who are fleeing abusive men in their homes. Women who are fleeing from attackers in police forces. Women fleeing retribution from individuals, and families, and communities, and governments, and militia, for simply being who they are. Most of the women in this group wanted to participate in the mock interviews, and as each of them went up for their turn, as I heard one story after another in rapid succession, it was chilling.

Each story sounded exactly like the one that came before it.

Even for a sympathetic witness like me, hearing the stories one right after the other made them congeal into a blob. Like they were all the same. Versions of the same. Which is true, I guess. There is a sameness to all our stories that should make the world realize the pervasiveness of its repeated injustices. But it is also a disheartening and disconcerting sameness that makes me wonder how the officers are going to be able to tell which of us is telling the truth and which of us is telling a lie. How are they going to be able to decide who to let in and who to keep out? How will they, the officer and the judge who

DOI: 10.4324/9781032685823-15

might have never lived or even imagined such circumstances, be able to look past the patterns and see the supremely individual swirls of our respective lives? If even someone like me can look at my peers' lives and see an undeniable sameness that makes me questions the lines between "authentic testimony and archetypal monologing" (I stole this expression from a friend here), how is a bureaucrat going to see us as unique individuals with unique lives, each of which needs its own time to be uniquely comprehended?

I didn't realize all this till I sat there, listening to the women's mock interviews back-to-back. One right after the other. One person after another. In much the same way that many of the people who decide our fates will experience us. One story after another. One narrative of suffering after another.

As I sat there, I found myself trying to evaluate the stories that were being shared by the mock interviewees in front me, and wondering whose suffering seemed more authentic. Wondering who seemed to be telling the truth. Wondering whose portrayal of suffering seemed most believable. And I'm on their side! I'm on their side and still, I found myself questioning if one story was more true than other. More real than another. More worthy of asylum than other. I had to stop myself, Chikki. I had to stop and remind myself that it didn't have to be one or the other. I had to remind myself that all their stories could be true. That all their/ our stories could be true, and that it didn't have to be a competition where only some of us could win.

I suppose that is the issue, though, isn't it? It *is* kind of a competition. How many of us will they let in? How will they judge our performance? Are their grading criteria flexible? What if I am an introvert who cannot cry in public? What if I come from a culture where pain is processed in silence? What if I am thinking so hard about the right words to use in English that I do not get carried away by the emotion of my own story (and it seems to be a given that they like to see displays of intense emotion)? What if I get distracted by the lights that are behind the interviewer's table? What if I am having a positive morning that day, on a rare occasion in which the past doesn't seem like it will get me down because of this, and I smile too much? What if I am having the worst day in the world, and can only speak in monosyllables? Will the officer who is interviewing me adapt their evaluation of my interview to allow for all these variables? Or will they simply apply the same criteria to each one of us, regardless of everything else? And if they are seeing us all through the same lens, how can this process ever be fair?

I guess that's why we practise.

I've been working on my own performance, and how I will tell my story.

The lawyer tells me that I'm glossing over the acid attack too quickly in the application and that I need to use more detailed images in describing what an acid attack looks like. That I need to try to articulate what it smells like. What it remains like on the skin of the body and the memory. Apparently, I have to paint the interviewer a picture of how acid burns through the skin and cuts through bone. Because if I don't do that, if I don't paint a picture with my words, if I don't also show them literal images of what my friend looked like after the acid attack, they won't understand how bad it all was.

How could an acid attack be anything but horrific? Why would someone need vivid descriptions and photos to prove how an acid attack can denigrate a person's physical and emotional being? My friend had acid thrown on her face. What else is there to say?

But they need more. So I've started thinking about how I'd describe the attack. How my friend was walking down the road minding her own business. How two men came by on a motorbike, flung something at her and left. How it all happened in the span of a few seconds. How her screams echoed through the neighbourhood for what seemed like hours afterward. How I didn't recognize her when I first arrived on the scene. How she lay writhing in pain till we were able to gain our bearings enough to call an ambulance. I'm trying to find the words to describe burning flesh. What it feels like to see skin shrivel and burn and dissipate in front of your eyes. Almost like watching meat being barbecued. What it feels like to focus on one part of your friend's neck because that's where the effects of the acid seemed to be slower. What it feels like to see the skin burn away and observe patterns emerge from beneath. What words would do justice to it, though? What words do I use to describe her screams or her pain or her new face? What can I say about a short period of time from which all I have are flashes? Do I make up more details? More than I can actually remember? Will they not believe me if I don't?

The real interview is coming up soon, in three days, so I'm trying to get all my ducks in a row. If things go well and the application is approved, I can start thinking about which city I'd like to move to and where I might like to start a life. But I'm trying not to get carried away thinking about that possibility. Because if things don't go well in the interview, I immediately get transported to a detention facility and held there till they arrange transport to take me back home. Apparently, I need to take my bags with me to the interview so that, depending on the verdict, I'm ready to go.

The asylum officer sits on a towering chair, behind a mahogany desk. It's dim in there. Blinds drawn on a sunny day. I enter the room from a lobby in which they've been playing a patriotic video on repeat. About the values of this country and all that it represents. Interspersed with commercials about a slow roaster that is great for cooking meat. I walk into the office with its artificial light and its piles of papers on the desk and see an officer who is different from anything I've imagined. I've imagined big burly white men mostly. Ones who have blond hair and blue eyes. Like Ken dolls in uniform. Instead, what I find is a sixty-year-old woman. Grey hair down styled in blunt cut. She is white. Frail. Wears glasses. She's shorter than me. Much shorter. She even looks dainty. And as she reaches out to shake my hand, all I see—all I can focus on—are her nails. Her nails that she has been clearly biting for years. The skin is peeling off the sides of her nails. They're red and chewed on and adorn hands that are scaly. Like the skin encasing them might fall off because it's so dry. Like snakeskin. Like parchment that needs to be doused in moisturizer. All I can look at her hands. The scaly skin and the bitten nails and the power that the exude over which way my application will go. "So you are here seeking asylum." All I can focus on are her fingers. As I reply to each of her questions, all I can look at, all that draws every bit of my attention, is the way in which her bitten fingernails are rubbing against the papers in my application folder. I answer her. I haven't forgotten the stakes. But it's hard to look her in the eye when all I can focus on are her hands. "I see that you feel your life is in danger if you continue to live in your home country. Tell me more about that." Staring at the peeling skin around the fingernail on the index finger of her right hand, I say something. All my practice goes out the window. None of my mock interviews had an officer with nails like that. With scaly skin like that. "Where did you live most recently?" I say something. "And that's where all of this happened and that's there you claim that your life is in danger?" I say something. Am I not making enough eye contact? "What about other parts of the country? It is a big country after all. Surely there are other places that you could move to, where you'd be safe? Places that are far away from where this all happened?"

I say something. Did I smile wryly? Is she going to misunderstand me? I want to ask her what she understands about spheres of influence where we're from. Does she understand that the people I'm running from have the kinds of connections that could follow me anywhere on that subcontinent? That these persecutors have such strong politically affiliated connections that all it would take is one phone call to unleash fatal consequences? Does she understand what it might entail for someone like me to move to the kind of small town or village where the bastards' contacts might be slightly less likely to tear my life apart? Do you know anything about the context that I come from, you finger-biting-skin-peeling motherfucker? "Tell me about the acid attack. It happened to your friend, yes? Nothing like that has happened to you? You have not been attached physically?" Running from a burning building that has been set ablaze by your persecutors doesn't count as physical damage, I suppose. The fear that keeps me awake at night, unable to eat, unable to sleep. The weight loss. The desire to self-mutilate. No, I don't suppose none of those things count in your definition of physical assault. These things are not graphic enough, are they? They are not violent enough? Pictures of my sleeplessness won't paint a painful enough picture of my fear, will it? They won't let you get off on the pornography of my trauma? You want to see bruises. You want to see mutilation. You want to see marks on my body that will make your torn fingers look like the petals of a lotus. "I'm sorry, but I don't see a credible fear here. I just don't see it." So I pick up my bags, walk back into the lobby, where meat is being smoked in a television commercial by a man wearing red, white, and blue. They put me in a room with a few others, where we are told to wait. Someone will come to take us to the detention centre.

My dreams these days are ominous, like a premonition, of sorts. Like my subconscious is trying to prepare me for impending doom.

My gut is telling me that this all going to go horribly wrong, Chikki, and I have no idea how to have hope. Whether having hope is more dangerous than not having any. Whether the illusion of possibility is simply going to cause a more fatal crash when it all comes crumbling down.

I know this has been all about me. I'm sorry. That's all I can think about right now. Myself. Where this is all going to end.

But, as a sign of good faith, that there's still a part of me that can consider others, here's a recipe for you. It's one that I've been making a lot over the last few days.

Refrigerator pudding

- butter—100 gms
- castor sugar—100 gms
- Marie biscuit or any similar biscuit—100 gms
- cashew nuts—100 gms (cut into small pieces)
- cocoa—two tsp
- egg—two
- brandy—two or three tbsp

Method

- cream butter and sugar well
- add beaten egg and cocoa
- crush the biscuit well (on a piece of paper) or in the mixie
- add the biscuit powder, cashew nuts, and brandy
- mix well
- fold in foil paper
- keep in the freezer till it sets
- cut into slices & serve topped with cream

I hope you are well and happy and enjoying every minute of the life that you've chosen.

I know you've spent the last few years questioning all your choices, wondering if you've made the right decisions, wondering if you should have walked down a different road. And a few years ago, C., I would have told you to leave. To leave him. To leave the life that you're questioning because life is too short to keep wondering what if. God knows I alluded to that more than enough times in my messages to you.

But I don't know anymore.

Life is too short for so many maybes.

Now I think that we make the best choices that we know how to make in a given instance and that maybe life is simply about making the best of those choices, rather than changing course to new ones.

Maybe there are some things that shouldn't be questioned, shouldn't be wondered about, shouldn't be missed, or romanticized.

Maybe there are some things that just need to be accepted for what they are. When they are. How they are.

Maybe that's all there is. The choices we make and how we live with them.

That's what I think today, anyway.

So, my dear, here's hoping that you find peace with the choices you've made. Whatever that peace might look like to you today.

I don't know where I'll be writing to you from the next time, Chikki.

I don't know when I'll write again.

F_

14 Interview five

A_ I thought about that. But it seemed like it wouldn't be, like, ethical, you know? To talk to someone who had been through . . . that. That's why, when P_ suggested that I speak with you, I just thought that, like, it would be a way to understand your students' experience, but without making them have to share all of that with a stranger.

X_ was a young boy, about twelve years old, whose parents had been caught by immigration officers for living in the country without the right papers. And during the time it took them to check the X_'s citizenship status, the officials had placed the child in detention. For months. This was not an uncommon story in the school X_ studied in. In one year alone, X_'s teacher has had over one hundred students face similar circumstances.

X_'s teacher has always known that the school he works in would be targeted for having a large number of students with lower income immigrants as its main parent body. X_'s teacher, R_, knows that the school is being targeted for being in the wrong part of town, where no families of influence live. When students start disappearing from a community that is already unseen, who is going to notice?

R_ knows that his students live in a constant state of anxiety. That some of them refuse to attend school because they are terrified of being not being able to be with their parents when enforcers show up for them. Not *if* it happens, *when* it happens. *When* it happens, when the government comes knocking at their door, R_'s students want to be able to be with their parents so that they can at least have the chance to say goodbye. No one wants to end up like X_: the twelve-year old who got picked up from school while his parents were at work. Yes, his parents were picked up too.

DOI: 10.4324/9781032685823-16

R_ knows that even students who do come to school are in no frame of mind to study. While their peers on the other side of the city prepare robust applications for the next step in their educational journeys, R_'s students are trying to make it through one more day without having their lives taken away from them.

A_ When they return, like . . . do they always return? I'm sorry, that didn't come out right. I mean to ask, like, do the students get held for a few months and come back to this school? Or do they get relocated? Do you stay in touch with them if they do?

R_ has too many stories to tell to A_. There are the students who come back, he tells her, as shells of themselves, unable to function in any capacity. There are students who come back, as if a fire has been ignited inside them, looking for a way to fight for their families and lives and their histories and their narratives. There are the students who come back sooner than their peers because they are lucky enough to find a competent lawyer. There are the students who disappear, never to be heard from again. There are the handful of students who return, pick up where they left off, graduate, and go on to do whatever they decide to do. Or whatever they can afford to do. Or whatever they are told to do. Or whatever they need to do. And there is the occasional student like X_. The student who never comes back but doesn't disappear. The one who calls after months of silence simply to say hello. The one who calls because he wants to let someone know, someone to whom his existence matters, that he is still out there. Somewhere.

R_ stays quiet for a long time after talking about X_, speaking again only when he is composed enough to articulate his guilt. His guilt and his helplessness. His guilt, his helplessness, and his impotence. R_'s guilt, helplessness, impotence, and complete loss of faith. In this country. In its government. In its laws.

A_ I cannot imagine what it must be like for you.
I'm so sorry. I—my mom—we've lost one person to this system and even that . . . it's been . . . I don't know how you bear it.
Is that where your work in the community has been helping? I heard that you have been helping your students organize, like, events in the community, to get their experiences heard?

I was wondering if you could share what you have learned from tha—those efforts. Like, what strategies have worked when you're trying to get people to care about what is happening to your students?

R_ begins with a clarification. The community-based attempts that he is organizing involve students of a different demographic. They do *not* include the students who are already afraid of being detained or investigated. He would never want to put such students through the stress of fighting for their lives in yet another way.

R_ tells A_ about how he crafts events that only involve students who are *not* at risk. Students who are *not* afraid of their families being pulled apart by immigration officers. And when R_ goes out with these students, they target communities like them. Communities that are safe(r). Communities that do not live with the fear of incarceration or deportation. R_ and his non-targeted students, he tells A_, show up to such communities and share a presentation that involves evocative storytelling—by the young people—about the friends that they have lost in the last year. Each member of the presentation team speaks about a student who had been taken away from their school: from a class; from a friend group; from a play's ensemble; from a sports team. Each student in the presentation team would speak about a peer who has been lost. A friend who has disappeared. A child who needs people like them, people who do not need to live with that kind of fear, to do more. Whatever this doing means to them. That is the goal of their presentations, R_ tells A_, to get their audiences to ask what it means for them to do something in the face of a humanitarian crises. Be it to donate. Or learn. Or protest. Or educate. Or organize.

R_ has many hopes for these presentations that are based in the importance of every single story; the singular story of every child he teaches; the singular story of every child that he doesn't. R_ has many hopes for what he wants to accomplish with his team of young storytellers: to foster an environment in which the immigration problem is not only for immigrants; to create a climate where the injustices of the carceral system are not only for the incarcerated; to build a community where the desire for a better life is not only a preoccupation for those in flight.

A_ And that's been . . . how do people respond when . . . you know . . . what's the general response been to the presentations?

"People mostly don't do anything." Sure, there is the occasional person who comes up to them at the end of their presentations and speaks about how moved they are to hear the students' words. A person or two who say that they want to help and that they will look into ways in which they could be part of the struggle. And for a few fleeting seconds such responses feel like a victory. But then what? What happens when these people go back to their homes? Probably the same thing that happens to R_ and his students when they go back to their homes. Their own lives happen. Their own families. Their own pains. Their own heartbreaks. Their own desires. And that's where it all inevitably falls apart.

R_ shares with A_ that he doesn't believe that his team's attempts at evoking action do much beyond making them—R_ and his student team—feel like they are doing something to be better allies and witnesses and companions and friends and peers and comrades. The only thing that they seem to be achieving, R_ shares, is something that helps them sleep a little better at night. Nothing more. Nothing less. His students are still disappearing, as are their parents; so, no, nothing seemed to be changing because of his attempts to get their stories out there. That being said, despite his acute awareness of the general futility of his actions in the face of a monstrous system that might well be inexplicable even for those who help create and maintain it, R_ and his student team keep at it. They keep going out. They keep telling singular stories. They keep trying to get more people to do whatever it is they are able and willing to. They keep doing this, R_ and his team of young storytellers, because that's all they know how to do.

That's all they can do. And they need to do something. To sleep a little better at night.

A_ I wonder what happened to the boy. The twelve-year old that he mentioned? I wonder where he is now.

Pause.

S_ I hear you and your dad went together the other day? To the detention centre?

Pause.

A_ I didn't know you two were talking again?

S_ We will always talk when it has to do with you. Always.

A_ It was . . . intense.

S_ He said it was a pris—centre hat only serves, you know, those—like—

A_ Trans asylum seekers? Yeah . . . It's the only detention facility in the country that has a separate cell block that's only for trans asylum seekers.

S_ I see.

A_ It was a big victory . . . like . . . it's so much safer for these women to have a block that doesn't have . . . you know . . . that's more secure and private.

S_ These are trans like from male to . . . you know . . .

A_ They are all trans women. Why ar—never mind.

S_ What?

A_ Nothing. I don't want to start an argument.

S_ It won't be an argument. Just tell me. We're trying to do this—us—differently, remember?

A_ Why are you so uncomfortable talking about this? You are part of the same community that these women are part of.

S_ I'm not trans—what are you saying, A_.

A_ Not trans. But you're gay. Or bisexual. Or pansexual. Whichever way you, like, however you identify . . . . because of . . . you're part of the queer community, no?
I just . . .
After everything that's happened . . . . I just don't understand . . .
How can you be so uncomfortable talking about this?
Even now?

Silence.

S_ It's only been a few months, A_.

A_ It's been years . . . hasn't it?

S_ I . . . I don't know how to ex —. . .

Silence.

S_ Do you remember how you cried when I took you to a circus for the first time? Because —

A_ —the horse's eyes were sad, yes, I remember.

S_ Imagine if I told you then that you were imagining it. That the horse actually wasn't sad and that you just needed to be

OK with what you saw in its eyes and get over your sadness. Would you have been able to do that?

A_ No, but how is that like th—

S_ I feel like I am the horse, kanna.

Your father looks at me and thinks he knows what the expression in my eyes is about. You think you see something. She thinks she sees something. But I'm the horse. I can't see what each of you thinks you're seeing. All I know is what I see and what I see is . . . unclear. Uncomfortable . . . You can't—even I don't know that my eyes are filled with right now. I don't know which experience . . . which memory . . . I don't know what's causing these things that everyone says they see in me. All I know is that I am like a horse that is in this circus and who has always been doing what it has been told to do . . . and one day, the horse is being asked what it wants to do . . . and it doesn't know. It just . . . maybe one day it will have a realization . . . an epiphany . . . . Maybe someday it will be able to . . . . able to separate its training from its desires and choose its own . . . road or path or whatever . . . . But it's also possible . . . it's likely that the horse will never know what it doesn't know how to know. It's possible that horse will forever do what it has been trained to do, even when it's been given the choice to do something different . . .

I think I'm losing track of my own ana —

A_ No.

No, I'm sorry.

You're right.

You're absolutely right.

That makes sense.

S_ It does?

It does, right?

Okay. Good.

Because . . . . Your dad told me that you once told him that you thought I didn't like you very much and I —

A_ No tha —

S_ No, it's OK, baby. You're allowed to think that. I understand why you think that. I've been . . . It's . . . .

You remind me of her. Not only in . . . you know . . . not only in how you are. But looking at you . . . . Every time I look at you,

it reminds me of the choices I've made in my life. How . . . .
Most days, many days, you remind me why I have this life and not another. Why I chose this life and not another. You . . . you are my anchor . . . .
But some days, sometimes, that reminder also means thinking about the life that I don't know how to imagine . . . . I think you can hear this now and understand that it has nothing do with you or how much I love you or —

A_ I know that.

S_ Good, because it has nothing to do with my loving you. Or him. It's just . . . I don't know how to grieve a life that I don't know if I ever could have had. With her.

A_ I . . . . I can't . . . . That sounds incredibly . . . I don't know if I have the right word.

S_ It's . . . . it's many things, darling. Half the time I don't know what I'm feeling and—Why did I even start talking about all this. I don't know.

Silence

A_ Still no news?

S_ They know she was admitted to a detention facility—her name is in the system. But they don't know if she is still there, or if she has been moved or deported . . . Apparently, their system is down.

Silence

A_ I really hope she's OK, Ma.

S_ Perhaps it's time I told you more about her. Maybe . . . Maybe I can start with why she calls me Chikki.

15 Part five

Your Safar

Safars are portals into another reality. When someone enters a Safar, they are transported into someone else's life for a few hours—one, five, twelve, twenty-four.

Safars are meant to be crafted carefully through research, from its creators' lived experiences, based in the grey zones of human experience.

Safars' Witnesses are meant to be carefully chosen so that the experience doesn't devolve into dark tourism.

Use the invitations below to build your own Safar.

- you can write directly into the spaces provided
- you can craft a Safar in a space of your choosing
- you can use the following link to engage with a collaborative, virtual space that has been created for the reader-writers of this book: https://tinyurl.com/WritinginBetween1. The same link can also be accessed by scanning the QR code

-f-f-f-f-f-f-f-f-f-f-f-f-f-

DOI: 10.4324/9781032685823-17

The suggested starting points below are simply that. Suggestions. Use them how you see fit. Edit. Redo. Repeat. It's your Safar.

This Safar is built by someone who

This Safar is built from research that

This Safar is built for Witnesses who

The Witnesses enter the Safar. They sit behind a glass wall where they can see in, but where those behind the glass cannot see out.

The time:

The place:

The Witnesses are asked to see

The Witnesses experience the smell of

The Witnesses are invited to taste

The Witnesses are made to feel

The Safar culminates when

-f-f-f-f-f-f-f-f-f-f-f-f-f-

Section 3

Between the personal and the political

Julys

1 Apoopa

Lights up.

Molay is twenty feet off the ground on a suspended platform that is made of white, flying seed clusters. She is enraptured by the flying tufts of hair-like substance, watching them, playing with them, reaching for them as they create an evocative image of a young woman floating on what can only be described as a cloud.

It is obvious that these white feathery creations are important to Molay. That they speak to her in some way.

And the only time she can look away from them is when the lights come up on the world below her.

Lights change.

Coimbatore. July 1985.

A bus stop.

Bus after bus honks loudly as each vehicle pulls into and away from the station where people are milling about: talking, laughing, solemnly pondering, eating molaga bhajis, smoking, drinking tea, staring, gossiping, and buying buns at Sun Star Bakery.

Amidst the hustle and bustle that occurs at that bus stop, every single day from 5:00 am to 8:00 pm, the lady in the green sari is a fixture. She is in her sixties or seventies, with all white hair that is pulled back in a messy bun. She is barefoot and hunched over in some combination of age and tiredness, with a patch over her left eye. As the buses get

DOI: 10.4324/9781032685823-19

in the way of other cars and rickshaws and cycles and pedestrians and cause traffic jams, the lady in the green sari pleads.

Lady in the green sari:	Amma, ayya. Amma, ayya. Amma, ayya. Amma, ayya.

Her hands are cupped, making the unmistakable sign that connotes begging for alms. Sometimes she is successful. Someone gives her 50 paisa; maybe a rupee here and there. The very rare person even takes the five minutes it needs to buy her a cup of hot tea and a packet of Parle-G biscuits from the bakery that's right behind the half-sheltered benches.

By and large, though, people act like they don't see the lady in the green sari. They ignore her at their air-conditioned car's closed window. They ignore her even when their windows happen to be rolled down, her voice nothing but a background score to their daily lives. They ignore her while they sip on their tea—sometimes apathetic, sometimes genuinely not seeing her, sometimes hoping against hope that she will simply walk away from them:

One person being asked for money:	So lazy these people are. Why can't they just get jobs, yaa?
Another person being asked for money:	This one has been at this bus stop for years, apparently. I heard she owns a begging business.
One person being asked for money:	Really?
Another person being asked for money:	Aamaa. They say she begs for money during the day, but she actually has this bungalow over there with many kids. That's what akka told me anyway. Maha killing she's making with this begging business.
One person being asked for money:	As if, yaa . . . maybe one person has given her 50 paisa in the last half an hour. How is she going to make any kind of profit like this?

Another person being asked for money: Who knows, da . . . . Maybe these are the kinds of stories that . . . you know . . . stories that we tell ourselves to make it easier to walk past her . . . Where there's no . . . enna solluradhu . . . logically we cannot understand the juxtaposition betwe —

One person being asked for money: Juxtaposition, ah? Fancy, fancy words yain use panaray?

Through all this hustle and bustle, it's almost impossible to see that there is a gateway that is snuggled in between the bus stop and the bakery that leads to someone's home: a two-storeyed structure with seven bedrooms, seven bathrooms, two living rooms, two dining rooms, and two kitchens. There are huge signs on the walls that line either side of this fifteen-foot-wide opening, naming the business owner and his two sons who own and live in the attached mansion. This almost hidden gateway leads into a car park that is home to four four-wheeled vehicles, with another gate that is off to the side, and that leads to a well cared for garden.

Tucked away at the very back of this car park, Apoopa is at his office table. Not the office-office that he goes to for the work that makes money. That office, the one that he uses to sell refrigerators, air conditioners, washing machines, and other home appliances—and that pay for this home—is a few kilometres away. No, this is his home-office: a bookshelf-lined room in the car park that Apoopa uses for the work he does for himself. The work of writing and translating stories and poems from Malayalam to English, from English to Malayalam. Works of passion that Apoopa, in his inimitable style, emotionally blackmails his press-owning friends to publish a small run of. Emotional blackmail that is followed by a careful manipulation of cultural codes which allow Apoopa to walk into the home of anyone who knows him and to leave having sold multiple copies of his latest creation.

Apoopa: This is my new book. How many copies can you print in the first run?
This is my new book. How many copies will you buy?

Questions that aren't really questions. Questions to which the potential publisher and purchaser have no choice but to respond to with a number. After all, who can say no to this business mogul who has come to Tamil Nadu from across the border in Kerala almost four decades ago, and who has built an empire from the humblest of beginnings? How can anyone in Coimbatore refuse to buy a book when the request comes from a stern, confident, wealthy, older man who has built his home with his own hands?

It will remain a lasting irony, of course, one that lasts well beyond Apoopa's demise, that despite all the acquaintances and friends who buy his books, read his books, support his books, his own grandchildren will never experience his writing. Because they are barely aware of his talents when they are young, and by the time his sons' four progeny are old enough to know and care and want to read their Apoopa's words, they cannot. Because Apoopa's grandchildren have never learned to read or write Malayalam.

As Apoopa sits in his office like he always does in the afternoons and evenings after returning from his work-for-money office, Molay—the version of her that is not floating above this Coimbatore of her imagination—is learning how to walk on the veranda that is right next door to her grandfather's office. The veranda with its white marble floors and ledges and steel benches and big open ceiling that is covered with a net and that is bordered with little star shaped light fixtures around its perimeter, multi-coloured little stars that light up birthdays and anniversaries and any other kind of celebration.

Molay is oblivious in the July of 1985, and remains tragically so for most of her grandfather's life, of what he is like beyond what she sees on the surface. All she sees is a stoic man, a successful man, an old man with an inimitably entrepreneurial spirit and a searing stubbornness that had prevented him from attending the funeral of his own father. What she will learn later, though, is that, as early as a year after her birth, while she was consumed by her appetite for milk and chocolate and sugar and everything related to those ingredients, Molay is already becoming the apple of her Apoopa's eye. He doesn't explicitly say anything about her being his favourite grandchild. After all, how can he claim to have one favourite when he has four of them living under the same roof. No, Apoopa doesn't say anything too obvious, but just from the way he looks at her, just from the way Molay behaves when she is around him, everyone knows that Molay is Apoopa's favourite. That's the word on the street.

A friend of the family: She's a lot like cheta, allay?
Molay's mother: You think so?
A friend of the family: Just look at her behaviour. Chetan da stubbornness aana atha.

Apoopa can't help smiling at this roly-poly one-year-old with her set of black milk teeth that haven't fallen out yet. Every time he looks at her, he cannot help but flash his characteristic smile. Warm. Hard to read. Quiet.

This time, in this July, things are no different. As Apoopa watches his granddaughter stubbornly go after the paper that's wrapping the cheese slice that she is trying to devour, he smiles. And as if she can feel his warmth, Molay walks over to him.

Molay: Thaa-di.
Apoopa: Endha Molay?
Molay: Thaa-di.

Pointing at her grandfather's stubble, Molay turns her attention from the cheese to the white flying seed clusters that are floating around them. White featherlike wisps that, in Malayalam, are aptly named "grandfather's beard."

Lights change.

The white tufts rise from the world on the ground to Molay's platform in the clouds, and Molay tries to capture each one in a bottle.

So that she can preserve it.

And label it.

And save it for a time when she will need to remember her grandfather.

Lights change.

July 1985.

Apoopa's affection for the youngest of his grandchildren is obvious. As obvious as the reality that he is a hard man to read, and that when displeased, he can be impossible to reason with. After all, this is a man who once took the societal expectation defying stance to not attend the last rites of his own father—in a culture and religion that glorifies the son's role in performing his parents' cremation, this one choice meant that Apoopa would forever be regarded with fear and admiration by strangers, by family, even by his wife.

Apoopa and his wife had had an arranged marriage more than three decades before the July of 1985, and things being what they were at the time, neither bride nor groom had had much of a say in the final outcome of the first meeting between their families. That being said, whatever the younger versions of themselves might have felt toward each other in the early days of their relationship, neither Apoopa nor Amooma talk about that time, ever. Even in the July of 1985. Maybe their silence can be attributed to the love that they soon found with each other, regardless of how the marriage came to happen. Or maybe they simply want to keep their emotions private. Or maybe Apoopa and Amooma don't talk about what they felt/feel because they do not understand marriages to be defined by feeling.

Whatever they might have thought or felt or considered at the time of their marriage, by the July of 1985, Apoopa and Amooma are a joint entity. He doesn't exist without her; she doesn't exist with him. Her husband might be the one to provide the money, but both Apoopa and Amooma and everyone else in the home know that she is the matriarch. And whether or not they have disagreements about how to run the household in the privacy of their room, these heads of household never show any discord in the presence of other family members living in the same home. All an outside eye will see is a husband committed to providing as much as he can for his wife, children, daughters-in-law, and grandchildren and a wife whose main worry is whether or not her husband has eaten enough to control the diabetes that he's had since he was twenty-five years old.

Apoopa's older son worries about how to keep his father's business alive while using it to build a new empire that will allow him to carve a niche outside of his father's shadow.

Apoopa's daughters-in-law struggle between deep respect and resentment for this patriarch. The one who had stopped these new additions to his family from studying further or from gaining employment that would take them outside the home.

Apoopa's second son, Molay's father, tries to keep up with running a business that was never something that he truly wanted to pursue. In the July of 1985, even as he leaves for the office before 8:00 am and returns after 8:00 pm, even as he burns the midnight oil trying to keep the business going, even as he tries to convince himself that Apoopa's path is his own and that he owes it to his father to carry on the family name, even as he does all of this, Molay's father wonders what life would have been like if he had had the chance to actually go to the United States for college.

Molay's father/Apoopa's younger son:	Acha, Sunny USla aana ippo.
Apoopa:	Good.
Molay's father/Apoopa's younger son:	He says that there are many opportunities there.
Apoopa:	Adhayo . . . good.
Molay's father/Apoopa's younger son:	Nyaanum apply chaiyatay?
Apoopa:	I built this business for you and your brother.
Molay's father/Apoopa's younger son:	I know, acha, but—
Apoopa:	Madi, monay.

In the July of 1985, Apoopa is a mix of terrifying and inspiring. His family is ever so slightly nervous about him. Around him. They are not so slightly intimidated by his ambition, his resolve, his temper. But they cannot help but be inspired by him. After all, it is only a handful of people in that generation, born into an era of colonialism and burgeoning post-colonialism, who could claim Apoopa's success story. His rags to riches tale of crossing state borders to start his own business is one of a kind—especially in a climate that wasn't/isn't welcoming of foreigners, even foreigners from within the borders of the same country. Stories that Apoopa never talks about; narratives that through his silence—because of his silence—manifest an intrigue around him.

Apoopa never talks about being born in 1919, the same year in which India was reeling from the Jallianwala Bagh massacre, a defining incident in which large crowds had gathered around pro-India independence leaders in Punjab and thousands were killed or injured by British troops. Apoopa never talks about living as a burgeoning businessman in the 1940s, as the northern and western parts of the subcontinent experienced a rupture that was entirely different from what its southern counterpart was experiencing. Apoopa never suggests that the Partition between India and Pakistan affected his life in any way—leading Molay to always wonder if the narratives that she came to learn later about the massacres and the tragedies and violations that defined the separation of India and Pakistan, even belonged to her individual history. What does it mean to be Indian when one's family's relationship to the creation of that nation-state is never acknowledged or named or identified or passed down?

Apoopa never talks about his past, and in this July, in the July of 1985, Molay is oblivious to the regret that she will feel many years later for never having asked for—or demanded—his stories.

Lights change.

On the platform, Molay is still immersed in capturing tufts of white seeds and trying to label their containers with notes for what each cluster might represent about her grandfather.

Time passes, though, and as it does, ensures that she cannot capture as many of the white clusters as she would like.

She is growing older.

Her changing body doesn't allow her to manoeuvre the floating cluster with the ease that she could earlier.

Holding on to the tufts becomes harder.

Twisting and turning on the hovering platform becomes less possible.

And soon, Molay finds that she has to start making choices. Choices about which tufts she wants to capture. And which ones she can accept—has no choice but to accept—letting go.

Lights change.

July 1991.

Molay and Apoopa's family home where—more than a decade before she will grow to hate the term "servants"—the grandfather and grandchild inhabit a world where multiple staff members do the things that the family members should, one might argue, be able to do for themselves. Of course, such an argument would be met with a litany of counterarguments by members of Molay's family.

Molay's aunt: It's part of our culture.
Molay's father: We are giving these people jobs.
Molay's uncle: If we didn't give them these jobs, they'd be languishing in godforsaken villages.
Molay's grandmother: This is all they know how to do.
Molay's mother: We treat them like family, so what's wrong with having help that we can afford?

It is the last of these justifications that Molay hears a lot. How the servants in their home are treated like family.

Family who eat leftovers while seated on the kitchen floor.

Someone else: In some homes, they won't even give them the same food that family members eat.

Family members who sleep on mattresses on the living room floor

Someone else: But look at the quality of the floor mats. And they can sleep on the drawing room floor or the kitchen floor. Or even the TV room floor if they want to watch a late-night movie.

Family members who are never allowed to leave the house except for errands that don't require more than a two-minute walk.

Someone else: It's for their own safety. All these bus drivers and auto drives are there, no? If one of our girls goes and has an affair with one of those fellows, that's all I need. Their parents will be here on the next bus demanding my head on a plate.

These family members are clearly different from those family members and yet the narrative around Molay is how well these family members are treated in this house compared to other places.

Molay is a sensitive child. She sobs as a five-year-old when she watches her aunt's wedding video because she feels, without knowing why or how, that the music playing in the background has a raaga composed for mourning and grief. Her heart melts every time the family's tailor smiles his white whiskered smile at her. But despite all this sensitivity, Molay does not question the whys and hows of the servants that she has had all her life. Why can't she make her own morning drink? Why can't she sweep the house? Why can't she clean the toilets?

It is a strange phenomenon. To be sensitive to things outside the walls of one's home and still be unable to see the tensions that lie within it.

Now, it's not like things between these and those family members are always defined by the more obvious power dynamics. In some ways, sometimes there is a strange form of camaraderie that is demonstrated between the two different kinds of family members in Molay's home. One of these family members, for example, confides in Amooma about the woes that she is experiencing with her husband who—she has come to find out—has an entirely different family with another woman. The woman who sweeps Molay's mother's floors shares with her employer that her in-laws keep bothering her for money—which is why she has to keep asking for advances on her salary. The woman who cooks for Apoopa's elder daughter-in-law speaks about a mother who is sick and ailing. One of the younger girls in the housekeeping team confides in Molay's cousin sister about the matrimonial matches that her family is setting her up on, and her hope that none of those matches will work out because she wants to find a way to study further. The woman who cooks for Apoopa's entire family has a bizarre relationship with Molay herself: part of a dynamic in which the 7-year-old child and the 40-something year old woman constantly antagonize each other with relentless questions and painful slaps on the other's arm. Of course, none of these female family members has a relationship involving the revelation of personal details with the men in the home. No, that would be immediate cause for gossip to spread. No, the male family members are only confided in by employees of the same gender. The drivers. The peons. The dhobis. The milkmen. The carpenters. The electricians. The plumbers. Yes, Apoopa and Molay's household has staff to take care of all those jobs too.

In the July of 1991:

6:00 am	Servant 1 is woken up by Apoopa's wife, Molay's grandmother. Servant 2 sleeps in a bit. Servant 3 sleeps in a bit.
6.30 am	Servant 1 wakes Servant 2 up after using the toilet that all three of them share in a house with seven en suite rooms, including several unused guest rooms. She puts the milk on to boil. Servant 2 wakes up and uses the toilet. Servant 3 sleeps a little bit longer.
7:00 am	Servant 1 makes morning drinks for the family while sipping on her morning tea. Servant 2 starts making breakfast while sipping on her morning tea. Servant 3 uses the toilet.
7.30 am	Servant 1 delivers the morning drinks. Servant 2 continues making breakfast.

	Servant 3 sets the breakfast table while sipping on her morning tea.
8:00 am	Servant 1 is on call to make hot dosas for breakfast.
	Servant 2 makes eggs to order.
	Servant 3 carries the hot food between the stove and the table.
8.30 am	Servant 1 eats her breakfast after the last round of dosas has been delivered.
	Servant 2 starts clearing the table.
	Servant 3 starts doing the dishes.
9:00 am	Servant 1 finishes the dishes.
	Servant 2 eats her breakfast.
	Servant 3 eats her breakfast.
9.30 am	Servant 1 starts working on lunch.
	Servant 2 dusts all the rooms.
	Servant 3 runs errands.
10:00 am	Servant 1 works on lunch.
	Servant 2 continues dusting all the rooms
	Servant 3 asks each family member if they want a mid-morning snack/drink.
10.30 am	Servant 1 makes midmorning orders.
	Servant 2 sweeps all the rooms.
	Servant 3 delivers the snack and drink orders as they get ready.
11:00 am	Servant 1 has her midmorning snack.
	Servant 2 continues sweeping all the rooms, with a mid-morning snack in between.
	Servant 3 has her midmorning snack.
11.30 am	Servant 1 continues cooking lunch.
	Servant 2 mops all the rooms.
	Servant 3 collects dishes from the midmorning snacks.
12:00 pm	Servant 1 starts prepping for dinner, to get ahead of some of the tasks that will allow her to watch an extra hour of TV in the evening.
	Servant 2 finishes mopping all the rooms.
	Servant 3 washes all the dishes and sets the table.
12.30 pm	Servant 1 talks to her estranged husband.
	Servant 2 watches TV, seated on the floor of the doorway of Apoopa's room.
	Servant 3 sneaks out of the house to meet her lover.

1:00 pm	Servant 1 makes the food that needs to be delivered to the table right off the stovetop. Servant 2 runs between the kitchen and the dining table, carrying that piping hot food. Servant 3 cuts the fruits that will be served at the end of lunch.
1.30 pm	Servant 1 has her lunch. Servant 2 clears the table. Servant 3 starts washing the dishes.
2 PM	Servant 1 finishes the post-lunch clean-up. Servant 2 has her lunch. Servant 3 has her lunch.
2.30 pm	Servant 1 naps. Servant 2 naps. Servant 3 naps.
3:00 pm	Servant 1 naps. Servant 2 naps. Servant 3 naps.
3.30 pm	Servant 1 wakes up to make everyone's afternoon tea/coffee. Servant 2 wakes up to make the evening snack. Servant 3 wakes up to go out and buy groceries and run any extra errands.
4:00 pm	Servant 1 has her evening tea. Servant 2 has her evening tea while continuing to cook the snack. Servant 3 delivers the tea to each member of the household.
4.30 pm	Servant 1 collects the used utensils from each household member. Servant 2 finishes cooking the evening snack. Servant 3 starts washing the dishes.
5:00 pm	Servant 1 starts preparing dinner. Servant 2 does the evening puja. Servant 3 sorts through all the clothes that the dhobi has brought back and takes them to each person's room.
5.30 pm	Servant 1 takes her evening bath while dinner cooks. Servant 2 calls her family. Servant 3 talks on the phone to her lover.
6:00 pm	Servant 1 can finally watch TV.

	Servant 2 takes her evening bath.
	Servant 3 continues talking on the phone to her lover.
6.30 pm	Servant 1 watches a movie, seated behind Apoopa, on the floor, in the doorway to his room.
	Servant 2 joins the movie watching brigade.
	Servant 3 asks everyone if they want something to eat or drink.
7:00 pm	Servant 1 watches the movie.
	Servant 2 watches the movie.
	Servant 3 brings people their evening snacks.
7.30 pm	Servant 1 watches the movie.
	Servant 2 watches the movie.
	Servant 3 starts setting the table.
8:00 pm	Servant 1 starts prep for dinner.
	Servant 2 sets the table.
	Servant 3 starts cutting post-dinner fruit.
8.30 pm	Servant 1 calls everyone for dinner.
	Servant 2 cooks the chapatis, puris, and anything else that needs to be prepared as the family sits down to eat.
	Servant 3 runs the freshly made breads to the table.
9:00 pm	Servant 1 starts cleaning the dishes.
	Servant 2 continues cooking as the family asks for things.
	Servant 3 starts clearing the tables.
9.30 pm	Servant 1 eats her dinner.
	Servant 2 finishes clearing the table and eats her dinner.
	Servant 3 does the daily accounting and grocery list-making with Apoopa's wife and Molay's mother.
10:00 pm	Servant 1 finishes the clean-up and goes to bed.
	Servant 2 eats her dinner before making sure all the doors and gates are locked and the bag is hung up for the milk man to make his early morning delivery before she finally lays out her mat on the living room floor to go to sleep.
	Servant 3 eats her dinner before sneaking off into the pantry to have phone sex with her lover.

In the July of 1991, Molay doesn't know to hate the word "servant" yet. She will. Soon.

Lights change.
July 1997 to July 2003.

An afternoon like so many before it, when the men have come home from the office, after a long day at the office. At lunch, the two brothers try not to address any of the topics that might lead to unnecessary disagreements, which are—as they both know—delayable but not preventable. They focus on the delicious mutton curry that is being served on their plates, with the straight-off-the-stove chapatis, which precede freshly made curd rice with pickle and pappadam, and are accompanied by their choice of room-temperature water or refrigerated water or warm water spiced with jeera and followed by freshly cut slices of Alphonso mangoes. Molay's father and her uncle make it through lunch without either of them mentioning any of the words that they know will set the other off. After all, these two men are just as similar as they are different. Similarly bull-headed. Similarly brash. Similarly sharp-tongued. Similarly loyal. Similarly generous. Similarly flawed. So similar in fact, that each brother feels the need to magnify and emphasize the differences they perceive in the other in order to convince themselves they are nothing like everything they abhor in their sibling. Just then, just as the plates have been cleared, just as their father suggests an afternoon siesta, just when it seems like the brothers are not going to get an argument this afternoon, in this July, someone says something.

Something innocuous.

Something vindictive.

Something manipulative.

No one knows to this day who exactly says the thing that provokes the one-line response that burns it all to the ground:

One of the brothers: What is it to you?

A line spoken by one brother to another; no one can remember which sibling said it.

One of the brothers: What is it to you?
The other brother: That's it. I'm done. I'm cutting off all ties with you.

That's it.

That's all it takes to end more than 40 years of being siblings.

At least for these two brothers.

When Molay comes back from school that day, she hears the news. That's all anyone is talking about.

Molay's someone: They have cut ties.
Molay: Who?
Molay's someone: Your father and your uncle.
Molay: They've done what?
Molay's someone: Cut ties.
Molay: What does that mean?

Molay is right to wonder what that means.

What does it mean to cut ties with someone who is biologically linked to you?

What does it mean to cut ties in a context where family is understood as being an unquestioned unit?

What does it mean to cut ties in a setting where loyalties framed by blood and marriage are considered binding, lifelong oaths?

What does it mean to cut ties when the people whose ties are being broken are two brothers—men who have been born to the same parents, grown up in the same home, studied in the same schools, and inherited the same business?

What does that mean?

No one knows on the day of that inferno in July 1997 what cutting ties means, but slowly, over the course of the months and years that follow, Molay comes to understand what the process entails.

Molay understands that cutting ties means Apoopa and his Amooma have to rewrite their will to accommodate the brothers' falling out. They have to meet with each of their sons at different times for the unforeseeable future, since both sons insist that a reconciliation is not possible. If that weren't enough, these tortured parents have to meet their sons' spouses and children separately too—the wives and children are not allowed to mingle.

Molay learns that cutting ties means that the family's patriarch and his wife will have to swallow their misery at seeing their two sons not talk to each other and that they will have to become accustomed to being treated like points on a business negotiation when it comes to demarcating what each son will inherit in each of their wills.

Molay learns that cutting ties means that Amooma and Apoopa will have to find ways to support each other through the kind of anguish that they never knew to expect. The kind of grief that comes from losing children while they are still alive. Apoopa begins to wonder if this is what karma is all about. If this is what his own father felt.

If her grandparents' experiences weren't material enough, Molay understands that cutting ties means that that her mother, brother, and Molay herself will have to promise their patriarch—Molay's father—that they will never speak to their aunt/ sister-in-law, their uncle/ brother-in-law, and their cousins, ever again. They will have to understand this new reality, whether or not they chose it or whether or not they understand what the feud between the two brothers is really about. Marriage and biology have chosen sides for them. And in order to remain on their side, in order not to get caught up in more cavernous twists and turns of family fracture, Molay, her brother, and her mother have no choice but to accept the way things are.

As months go by, Molay understands that cutting ties means that she and her brother cannot attend their cousin sister's upcoming wedding or their cousin brother's graduation. No, the kids cannot have one last conversation with their aunt, who—the last time they saw her, a week before the brothers' fight—had generously hosted a slumber party at the new mansion that their uncle's family had moved into a year or so before . . . Molay, her brother, and her mother will understand that cutting ties means swallowing any nostalgia, any remorse, any recriminations, any desires because—like his own father—Molay's father is simultaneously sensitive and terrifying. Yes, he will be heartbroken if any one of them breaks the code of silence that he has demanded. Yes, he will not take their betrayal in silence.

Molay understands that cutting off ties means that the two brothers have to learn to ignore the tears and the pleas of everyone who tries to patch up their relationship. Friends. Parents. Wives. Children. Tears. Recriminations. Reasoned arguments. Explosive diatribes. Informed interventions. Emotional stipulations. Drunken conversations. Seductive manipulations. The two brothers have to learn to let none of it affect what they have decided to do. They have to learn not to listen to anyone but themselves.

Molay understands that cutting off ties means both legal and emotional separations. Her uncle and father even go so far as to make an announcement about their split in the newspaper lest anyone in their city think that their respective halves of the business—that their father had started from the ground up and that they had inherited for no reason but the fact that he was their father—were actually part of the same unit. The same family. The same empire. The same bloodline.

Molay understands that her father and uncle have to tell themselves that their respective manic, bipolar conditions have nothing to do with how they handled the argument that day. They have to let go of any attachment to logic to convince themselves to not see that they are nothing more or less than troubled men who have let years of resentment and unresolved tugs of power affect the future course of not only their own relationship, but the ones between their two households. They have to learn to quiet the voices in their head that tell them that the catalytic afternoon could have been handled differently. That maybe "What is it to you?" could have been responded to with "fuck off," or "it's my business too," or "I need a smoke break before we can talk more," or anything. Literally anything except, "I'm cutting off all ties with you."

As years go by Molay understands that—if her father's and uncle's cutting ties is any indicator—there are likely no earthly bonds that are unbreakable. That there might not be any kind of love that can be fully unconditional. She will, for the rest of her life, ask herself this: if my father can cut off his brother, is there something I can do which will make him cut ties with me? Molay will, for the rest of her life, have to wonder that if the love between brothers has a breaking point, is there any kind of love that doesn't?

Perhaps it's no surprise then that in the July of 1997, Molay watches Apoopa with more attention than she usually does. In the early hours of this morning, for as long as her father and her uncle remain with their ties cut, a similar scene plays out. Molay's father has his morning coffee with his parents in their room, every single day. And as he sits there, as shlokas play on the tape recorder and praise a multitude of Gods—sometimes in the voice of his former brother's wife—the conversation eventually returns to their sons' broken relationship. For years after the brothers had made the decision to sever their relationship, Molay hears her grandparents attempts at counselling their younger son. To advise him. To cajole him. To plead with him.

Apoopa:	Forgive him, monay. You're brothers.
Molay's Father:	Just because we're brothers, it doesn't mean we have to be in each other's lives forever.
Apoopa:	That's exactly what it means.
Molay's Father:	Come on, acha. You didn't go to your father's funeral.

Molay sees the change in Apoopa's demeanour from the moment ties are cut off between his two sons. He begins to carry a load, a load that sometimes shines through as anger. Sometimes as an even more ardent withdrawal into silence. Sometimes, in the darkness of nights that can only be imagined since no one but his wife is privy to them, a load that manifests as heaving sobs that threaten to break Apoopa's bones.

Molay watches Apoopa's struggle with his sons' estrangement take on different forms in different Julys. The particular shade of Apoopa's pain in the July of 1998 when the first of his grandchildren gets married without any of his younger son's family in attendance. The tone that his torment takes on in the July of 1999 when his sons finish the legal and financial tearing apart of the business that he has built with his blood, sweat, and tears. The intensity of Apoopa's dilemmas in the July of 2000 when his older son suffers a stroke that leaves him paralyzed—a physical, emotional, and psychological disintegration of Molay's uncle that finally leads to a reconciliation between the two brothers.

A reconciliation that occurs because Molay's father sees that his older brother is no longer himself. This version of his brother, the one with his slurred speech and weak body and inability to physically take care of himself, is nothing like the firecracker with whom ties had been cut with a simple "What is it to you?" Gone is the brash, confident man of the world whose perceived arrogance and sharp tongue used to get under his younger brother's skin. Gone is the man who has no compunction throwing money at a problem and at loudly listing his successes. Left, in his place, is someone who needs his wife to act as a translator. Left, is a man who cannot eat or walk or stand or lay down without assistance. And if Molay's father is only able to forgive his brother because he views him as a shell of his earlier self, one must wonder: what kind of reconciliation is that?

In the July of 2003, when Molay comes home for a two-week holiday from college in the United States—her Apoopa looks emaciated, worn out, and fatigued. Perhaps this is what happens when one watches their children reject their brotherhood. Perhaps this is what happens when the business one has built has been broken apart in a way that can never be put back together. Perhaps this is what happens when one's spouse of multiple decades develops ailment after ailment, making husband and wife realize that their time together is finite. Perhaps this is simply the way of life . . . vitality and youth crumble over time to create versions of selves that are barely recognizable.

When Molay manages to come back to visit her grandfather in the July of 2003—her first visit home after becoming an international traveller; after seeing countries that Apoopa doesn't know exist—she immediately notices how hollow he has become. The sunken-ness of his skin. The way his already sparse speech has almost stopped. The way his eyes seem to have acquired many more bags and lines around them. The way his used to be sharp memory has dimmed.

Apoopa: That used to be ours, Molay.
Molay: I know, Apoopa.
Apoopa: Nyagalday business.
Molay: I remember.
Apoopa: Ellam poyi.

Apoopa and Molay return to silence in the backseat of a car, as they are driven by the showroom that—at one point in their lives—represented the success of the patriarch's skill, determination, and success. The two-storeyed, glass windowed structure in one of Coimbatore's most commercial areas, where Apoopa had sold fancy household appliances.

Surrounded by the sound of July's monsoons the words "All gone now" echo in Molay's ears as she and her grandfather silently watch the building disappear in their car windows.

Apoopa and Molay sit in silence.

Not necessarily mourning the losses.

Not necessarily sad for what has changed.

They sit in silence because that is what has defined most of their relationship.

Silence that is punctuated by poignancy.

Silence broken by words that will replay in Molay's heart long after her Apoopa no longer has an earthly manifestation.

Silence that encompasses their love for each other in ways that neither will ever understand.

Apoopa: That used to be ours, Molay.
Molay: I know, Apoopa.
Apoopa: Our business.
Molay: I remember.
Apoopa: Ellam poyi.

When the car reaches its destination, Molay and Apoopa continue to sit by each other. She reaches out to him, takes his hand in hers and kisses the back of it, like she always does. He smiles quietly, lets his hand squeeze hers before taking it back, like he always does.

They sit by each other in the parked car. Grandfather and granddaughter. Two people who adore each other in ways in that they never quite fully understand.

Even when they arrive at their destination in this afternoon of July of 2003, they continue to sit by each other.

Silent.

Content in the quiet.

A quiet content.

Granddaughter, grandfather, and everything their bond is made of.

Apoopa: That used to be ours, Molay.
Molay: I know, Apoopa.
Apoopa: Our business.
Molay: I remember.
Apoopa: All gone now.

Lights on both versions of Molay.

The monsoons take over everything. The water drenches the earth and everything on it. It rises and rises and rises and rises till it reaches Molay's floating white seed cluster bed. It stops there, the water. It stops when it reaches the edges of the floating platform. The monsoons stop. The rising stops. And as Molay stands on her white cluster bed looking into the flowing currents beneath her, it is the July of 2010 and her Apoopa's ashes are being immersed in both the river of her imagination's making and the banks of the one on Coimbatore's outskirts where she had stood that morning.

As Molay watches the flowing currents beneath her, it is that morning, a month after Apoopa died; two weeks after he said he had seen Yama, the God of Death, appear in his dreams; a few months after Molay had last seen him and tried to ask him all the questions she had never thought to ask before, almost exactly five years after the death of his beloved wife.

Molay stands on the banks of the river and watches as the men of the home follow the instructions of the pujari on what they must do and say and how they must do it and say it before immersing Apoopa in the waters that will take him away. And as she watches, she believes,

Molay does, that Apoopa might have wanted her to be the one to perform his last rites. That he might have wanted—if he had any choice in the matter—his favourite granddaughter, the one who was becoming more and more like him each day, the one with whom he shared an explicable bond, the only grandchild who was present at this funeral . . . Apoopa might have wanted Molay to be the one to send him off into the afterlife that he never fully believed in.

But, of course, tradition doesn't allow that.

Customs don't allow that.

Religion doesn't allow that.

Ritual doesn't allow the female grandchild to be the one to set her grandfather off into whatever does or does not lie ahead.

So all that both versions of Molay can do is watch.

From the banks of a river Molay watches as this man she knows but doesn't, is like but isn't, wants to become like but doesn't, washes away.

Molay, on the white seed tuft platform

Molay, on the banks of Coimbatore's holy tributary

Both these Molays watch as the last physical remnants of Apoopa's body wash away.

All gone now.

Lights down.

2 You

Part one

Let's bring up the spotlight on you now.

Yes, you.

I want to invite you to take a journey across your own realities and imaginations, through your own versions of yourself, with those who might be your Apoopa. Or Maestro. Or Amma. Or My Dear. Versions of yourself with those you know—and who know you—intimately. Versions of yourself with those you might have only met in a book. Versions of yourself with people you do not know in any tangible way but have always wished to engage with. You don't even have to choose a person. Perhaps you want to reflect on versions of yourself within the context of a place. Or a concept. Or the lyrics of a song.

In such speculative recollections of pasts that are as real as they are imagined, as factual as they are magical, it is the process of filling in the gaps that is revelatory. Enriching. These are journeys that have guideposts but not destinations; hopes rather than goals; journeys that are as actual as they are fantastical, as honest as they are fictional. Choose a version of yourself with someone that matters. A real version of you with an imagined someone else. An imagined you with a real version of someone else. A somewhere between the two version of yourself with a somewhere between the two version of someone else.

What's your choice?

- you can write directly into the spaces provided
- you can write in a space of your choosing
- you can use the following link to engage with a collaborative, virtual space that has been created for the reader-writers of this book: https://tinyurl.com/WritinginBetween2. The same link can also be accessed by scanning the QR code

DOI: 10.4324/9781032685823-20

Next, after you've chosen a version to focus on, ask yourself what this version of you might be doing within the context you've chosen. What is the chosen version of yourself looking at or listening to or thinking or feeling or eating or smelling or imagining or something else-ing? Is this doing, whatever it is, real or surreal or allegorical or theatrical or just plain absurd? Where is this version of yourself located: a physical space, a geographical location, a metaphorical frame, an inebriated illusion? Who or what is this version of yourself alongside: something human or non-human? Perhaps a philosophical idea?

Remember, you have absolute permission to bend and stretch the boundaries of this invitation. People don't have to be humans and places don't have to be physical; the real doesn't have to be the realistic, and the imagined doesn't have to be fathomable.

- you can write directly into the spaces provided
- you can write in a space of your choosing
- you can use the following link to engage with a collaborative, virtual space that has been created for the reader-writers of this book: https://tinyurl.com/WritinginBetween2. The same link can also be accessed by scanning the QR code

3 My dear

Lights up.

Underground. Beneath the translucent red earth of Rwanda.

Dinesh is digging up, light emanating from a source that cannot be placed.

The underground is cavernous. Made of intertwined roots. And rocks. And cobwebs. And bones.

Here, Dinesh seems simultaneously far and not so far from Rwanda. From My Dear.

She digs frenetically, digging with a seeming desperation. And as her efforts intensify, so does the light.

Freneticism +10	Luminosity +10
Freneticism +20	Luminosity +20
Freneticism +30	Luminosity +30
Freneticism ++++	Luminosity ++++
	the light blinds
	Bursts into darkness.

Silence.

We hear the digging stop. We sit in the darkness. Silent darkness punctuated by something like the sound of eggshells breaking. Maybe she is scratching herself. Maybe she is crawling to find a comfortable spot. Maybe she is stepping on bones.

DOI: 10.4324/9781032685823-21

It begins almost like the flicker of a candle; the return of the light does. A small flame. Yellow. Warm. Different from the starkness of what came before.

As Julys pass, the flame becomes a burn becomes a simmering. She is digging more thoughtfully now. Digging with something that can only be described as care. She is being careful. With the rocks. And the roots. And the cobwebs. And the bones.

Especially the bones.

She scrutinizes each object that she moves. As if she is trying to imbue them with some kind of meaning. Like she is asking herself where the rock came from. What caused the gravel to take on particular shapes and sizes and colours and edges. Why the cobwebs are stitched together here but not there. And as she lifts each bone with a delicate respect, it is like she is trying to ask each of them to tell her their tale. "How did you get here?"

Maybe she is not supposed to be making her way to the surface after all, Dinesh thinks to herself. Maybe she has just been reacting based on some impulse which tells her that staying underground is less desirable that being above it. Maybe she has just been indulging unquestioned assumptions that have been telling her brain and her body to *do* because doing something is better than doing nothing. But maybe that's not the case.

Maybe sometimes, many times, Dinesh wonders, doing nothing is the better choice. The best choice. Maybe sometimes, many times, nothing should be done because nothing can be done.

Nothing should be done.
Nothing can be done.

Because there are things that happen which warrant the world coming to a stop.
A pause.
A silence.
If, for no other reason, than as an acknowledgement that nothing should ever be the same again.

And so, Dinesh stays still.

A stop.
A pause.
A silence.

Nothing must ever be the same after the 1994 genocide in Rwanda.

Nothing should have ever been the same after the peace accords were signed in Guatemala in 1996.

Nothing would ever be the same after the communal riots that shook Coimbatore in 1997.

Dinesh starts to wrap the underworld around herself—she starts to wrap herself in the underworld—till everything seems like an extension of her. Roots flow out of her arms. Leaves adorn her bosom. Bones go through her, into her, out of her—warped branches of white calcium that glisten like threads sown to hold together different pieces of the whole.

The wrapping around/within/through continues for so long and so seamlessly that by the July of 2013, Dinesh is indistinguishable from the world around her, beneath her.

She becomes it.
It becomes her.

Lights change.

July 2013.

Kashmir.

"Why don't Indians care about Kashmir?" a spectator asks, refusing to let his responses be restricted to the world of the performance that Dinesh has co-created with colleagues turned friends. He doesn't care about the play he's just engaged with, no; this audience member wants to accuse, to vilify, to avenge. No matter how insignificant this act of vengeance might be in the grand spectacle that is the Indian nation-state's presence in the Kashmir Valley.

Dinesh: Clearly, I care. That's why I'm here.
Spectator: Sure, you're here now. How long will you stay?

Dinesh returns to her room in tears. She wants to scream at her critic for lumping her in with a general category of "Indian" who doesn't care about Kashmir. She wants to scream at this man for wanting to incriminate when she has come to his home to create art. She wants to tell him to fuck off, that he has no right to question her intentions without having ever spoken to her about why she does what she does.

He doesn't know how much soul-searching has underpinned Dinesh's decision to make Kashmir the space for her work after the less than ideal outcomes of her attempts in Kigali. He doesn't know how much thought she has given to her insider-outsider positioning in the valley and how this identity might allow her the kind of connection and distance that she never had in the land of a thousand hills. He has no idea how many discomforts Dinesh has endured in the creation of this unique piece of theatre that he has just experienced; hours and days and months and years in which Dinesh has tried to channel every lesson gathered from her times in Guatemala and Rwanda and all the stops that came between them.

Dinesh wants to tell her critic all this.

Accuse him of all this.

Throw his words back at him.

But she can't.

All she can seem to do is return to her room, sobbing.

In the July of 2013, when Dinesh feels misunderstood in Kashmir, when her intentions are questioned and insulted by strangers, she is affronted. Offended. Hurt.

It will take her many more Julys, almost a decade of them, to realize that one of the reasons her critic's words might have stung so deeply that day is because there was truth to them.

On that day in July 2013, Dinesh's critic was right to remind her that being here now did not mean that she would return or continue to care. Maybe Dinesh's critic was right to say what he did because Kashmir, like Rwanda, has had a never-ending stream of well-intentioned outsiders coming into the homes and hearths of its peoples only to disappear when the going gets tough. Well-meaning, generous outsiders who are never fully able to grasp—or contend with—the privilege that comes simply with choice. The choice to come to this place. The choice to witness its layers. The choice to ask questions about its pain. The choice to engage with its stories. And, of course, the most important one, the choice to leave. Maybe her critic's words wound Dinesh in the July of 2013 because she knows that the thing he is pre-emptively accusing her of doing in Kashmir is exactly what she did in Rwanda. To Rwanda. To My Dear.

They have completely lost touch by now, Dinesh and My Dear. It's almost as if ever since Dinesh realized—less than eighteen months after her first departure from Kigali—that there was no place for her in Rwanda, no place for Rwanda in her, a switch has been turned off. By the July of 2013 these two young women exchange an odd message once or twice, where My Dear writes to ask Dinesh when she'll be coming back. Where My Dear writes to tell Dinesh that the members of the theatre ensemble have asked about the next festival they are going to do together. Dinesh will never be able to explain it very well to anyone who asks, "Why haven't you gone back to Rwanda?" "How are your colleagues and friends there?" "What are they up to?'" All Dinesh can do every time she is asked a variation of these questions is look away. Ashamed. Nostalgic. Regretful. What else is there to do?

Dinesh has a difficult time answering such questions even when she is the one doing the asking. She doesn't entirely know why she has never gone back to Rwanda. Why, in July of 2013, it has been more than four years of radio silence between her and the place that once was the most important aspect of her life.

She does have some hypotheses, though:

Maybe part of her complete disconnect from Rwanda has to do with shame. How can she not be ashamed? After all, for more than a year, Dinesh had been convinced—to the bone, to the soul—that Kigali would be her new home. For more than a year she had been convinced, with every fibre of her being that making theatre in Rwanda was her calling, that it was going to be her way to make a difference in this world. For more than a year she had told everyone in her life about the man she had fallen head over heels for while she had been in Rwanda, a man that she thought she knew in her gut that she was going to "end up with." How could she not be ashamed that it all amounted to nothing?

Maybe part of Dinesh's complete disconnect from Rwanda just has to do with time. Time passes. People move. Lives change. And that is simply—in all its inadequacy—the entire extent of why some relationships that feel like they will extend across all fathomable representations of space, simply come to an end. Maybe disconnects are simply part of life, who we are, who we will become. Nothing more. Nothing less.

Or maybe, just maybe, disconnects are about ensuring that the beauty of what once was is cherished for everything it used to be, rather than being diluted by futile attempts to carry it on into the future in ways that would dishonour the authenticity of the original. Perhaps the mind and heart's ability to disconnect—however inconsistently, however sporadically—is the body's intrinsic way of making space for the new. A way of making certain that the weight of the past is carried with just a little more ease.

Maybe disconnect isn't disconnect at all, but just a shift into absence. A shift into memory. A shift into the imagination.

Maybe disconnect is not a break, but an absorption. An integration. An assimilation. A process in which what was once an entity outside of the self becomes indistinguishable from it.

Maybe there is no such thing as disconnect when speaking of people and places and ideas and things that shape our souls.

Memories become us.

We become them.

Lights down.

4 You

Part two

Next, with your chosen version of yourself, within the situation that you've defined further, add the element of time. Maybe you'll choose a July. A July from this year. From that one. One from the past or one from an imagined future. Or maybe you will choose a different month altogether. Maybe Octobers are more your speed. Maybe you don't want to think of time in months and would prefer to consider a specific day of the week. Or a particularly significant date. Maybe you are not constrained by these forms of time and have, instead, a completely different understanding of it. The choice is yours.

- you can write directly into the spaces provided
- you can write in a space of your choosing
- you can use the following link to engage with a collaborative, virtual space that has been created for the reader-writers of this book: https://tinyurl.com/WritinginBetween2. The same link can also be accessed by scanning the QR code

DOI: 10.4324/9781032685823-22

Once you've made the choice, your temporal choice, consider how you will connect the dots between your chosen version of yourself, your accompanying people, ideas, locations, actions, and the time that you've decided to explore. Can they be connected through what was happening in that world at that particular moment in time: a cultural phenomenon, a historical occurrence, or a political reality? Do the dots even need to be connected? Is connection a construct that feels unnecessary? Are fragmented episodes a more authentic representation of your experiences of the world?

- you can write directly into the spaces provided
- you can write in a space of your choosing
- you can use the following link to engage with a collaborative, virtual space that has been created for the reader-writers of this book: https://tinyurl.com/WritinginBetween2. The same link can also be accessed by scanning the QR code

5 Maestro

Nandita Dinesh

Lights up.

Mi Amor is sitting cross-legged inside a structure made of letters, letters from the alphabets of Tamil and English and Malayalam and Hindi and Spanish. The letters flow in streaming vertical lines, in a loop, like pixelated code on a computer screen.

As Mi Amor looks and observes and investigates and considers the letters that stream all around her, it's like she is trying to create new vocabularies. Mixing and matching. Matching and mixing. Across, between, through the different alphabets that articulate who she might be becoming.

But the thing is . . . the thing is that Mi Amor can only do that much. Only that much mixing and matching. Only that much across-ing and between-ing. Only that much because her head is held in a vice. A steel contraption that is wound so tight that it locks her gaze right in front of her. Close to her. Making it impossible for her to see anything that lies beyond a very narrow field of vision. Looking beyond what the vice allows could make her eyeballs explode from the pressure.

Mi Amor is so obsessed with constructing new words and ideas that she cannot see the extraordinary colours around her. Greens that slowly turn into browns and yellows and oranges and rusts. A mosaic of colours that, if recognized, might encourage Mi Amor to think about how to loosen the vice. A palette that, if acknowledged, might allow her to see the streaming letters from an angle that also widens the scope of her vision.

But no.

Mi Amor, in this moment, in this space, is constrained by the vice, her words, and what she can do with them. What they can do to her.

DOI: 10.4324/9781032685823-23

Mi Amor doesn't see the images that unfold beyond her container. She cannot see what happens around her because the vice consumes every ounce of energy in her body.

Mi Amor wants to try to make more words—new words, mixed words. She wants to create new ideas—better ideas, mixed ideas. Words and ideas that might capture the depths and layers to what she is feeling and who she is becoming,

But she cannot.

All she can feel is the vice getting tighter. Like someone or something is tightening the rod on the clownishly monstrous C-clamp that crowns her head.

Someone. Something. Turns the rod. A quarter of an inch to the right.

Righty-tighty, lefty-loosey.

A quarter of an inch to the right.

That's all it takes.

She can feel the blood rushing harder, like waves on a shore during high tide.

She can feel the pulse at the corner of her forehead become inseparable from her mind's wailing.

She can see fewer letters now. Fewer and fewer and fewer and fewer. Just keeping her eyes open is a gargantuan task.

As the greens and reds and rusts and oranges around her shine and dance and celebrate and evolve, all Mi Amor can do is try not to keel over from the pressure that has resulted from a quarter of an inch right turn on the handle of the clamp on her head.

Righty-tighty, lefty-loosey.

The letters have fallen down now. They lie at Mi Amor's feet.

Letters made of sharp edges and pointed spears. Letters like shards of glass.

The type of foliage that fractures colour and creates starkness.

Mi Amor sits amidst the shards.

It's almost like she cannot stop herself. Like the pressure on her head makes it impossible for her not to be drawn in by the letters' sharded potential as instruments of pain.

It's like the vice is telling her to do this. Making her do this.

Pain making the possibility of more pain seem seductive.

Necessary.

She picks up one of the letters and begins to carve her feet with them.

Designs that replicate the mehndi patterns that she has grown up observing. Intricate designs. Detailed designs.

Designs that cannot be fully seen through the blood their etching leads to, but ones that Mi Amor knows are there.

When she is done with her feet, when they are as embellished as they are mutilated, Mi Amor picks up a different letter. From a different language's alphabet. And begins on etch on her stomach this time. An outline.

A map of her many homes.

A map of the many places she has called home.

Mi Amor continues this practice—an almost ritual—until her entire body is covered in tracings made from sharp pointed edges.

Until she is inseparable from the patterns.

Until she is inseparable from the blood.

Once she has embellished her body in a way that satisfies the unnameable thirst that she has been trying to quench through her actions, Mi Amor begins to stand up from amidst the weaponized letters that are strewn around her.

As she does, as she stands up fine, glass-like dust falls from the newly created markings on her skin. In her skin. Glass-like fine dust, from the knife tips that she was using on herself.

Silver confetti.

Bejewelled blood.

Remnants.

The vice is gone now, and all that remains on her head, on her body, are wounds. Not that long ago to have become scars. Not too recent to be wet to the touch.

Wounds on her head, wounds on her body. Semi-dry wounds. The kinds of wounds that have no choice but to leave marks.

Wounded, marked, and covered in caking off dry blood from those parts of her body that have not formed gashes, Mi Amor—finally—notices the colours.

She can see the greens now.

And the rusts.

And the reds.

And the oranges.

She can finally see the colours of autumns she has never known.

She can see the world outside now.

The Guatemalas.

And the Rwandas.

And the Indias.

She can finally see glimpses of the outside without being eaten away by what's within.

Finally,

eventually,

slowly,

Mi Amor thinks she just might be able to try again.

She picks up the fallen alphabets, one letter at a time, and tries to set them back up.

Off the ground.

Neither as the bars they were before, nor as the carving knives they became later.

Mi Amor re-installs and de-installs and re-installs again.

Trying to find a new structure to capture the shifts in her understanding of language.

Lights change.

For many, many Julys after their farewell, Mi Amor will recall the silence of the final hours that she spent in Maestro's presence. The silence that engulfed the 20-something-year-old woman/ student/ mentee/guest and the 40-something-year-old man/ artist/ guerrillero/ host who are sitting in silence, on a bus, right next to each other. The silence that is punctuated by moments in which she awakens between fits of slumber to look over at him and make overtures to break the stillness. The very fraught quiet. To get him to help change the tone of their goodbye. To make this not be the way in which they last see each other. Maestro doesn't speak to Mi Amor again until the bus reaches its destination in Guatemala City and they are forced to sit across from each other at the only 24-hour diner that they can wait at until the taxis begin their morning shifts.

Maestro: That night, when I tried to kiss you, you said you didn't want to return it because you didn't want to enter into anything while you have a life on the road.

Maestro speaks after eight hours of silence of having understood Mi Amor's rejection of him that night as a rejection of all interactions with a hint of romance. He tells her of having understood her rejection of him as being caused by her decision to not enter into any type of romantic intimacy with anyone, while she was travelling as much as she was at the time. He doesn't think, for a moment, that Mi Amor is simply rejecting a romantic liaison with him.

Lights flicker.

> Even as Mi Amor re-installs and de-installs and re-installs the letters again, even as many Julys pass after her farewell from Maestro, he is a constant presence in Mi Amor's negotiations with the world.

Lights flicker.

When Mi Amor returns to graduate school in the July of 2007, immersed in intellectual masturbation about theories of memory and trauma, she often wonders what Maestro would say about inaccessible academic theories that cannot be read or understood by the very people they are supposed to be written about or for. When she moves to Rwanda in July of 2008 to start a theatre company there, Maestro's words replay in her head: "If you're truly trying to help artists in war zones, find a way to do that from the outside." When she is back in India in the July of 2009, she can hear his voice: "I told you. There's no place for outsiders in something like this." When she is in Mexico in the July of 2010, she wonders if she has the money to go over to Guatemala to see her Lake Atitlan again. When she is in Coimbatore in 2011, being treated for a panic disorder, she sees him in her dreams. Maestro. His eyes. He's there. And as part of the therapy she is undergoing to numb the searing fear that is pummelling through her every second of every day, she is remembering all the moments from her past in which the seeds of that anxiety might have been sown. Or watered. Or nurtured. And of course, her last night with Maestro is one of those seeds that forms a small, sturdy, integral part in what becomes a viny, intertwined network of stimuli that foster depersonalization and derealization and shortness of breath and fear.

> *Lights flicker.*
>
> Mi Amor re-installs and de-installs and re-installs the letters.
>
> Trying to find a new configuration that captures her shift in the understanding of language.

Lights flicker.

Mi Amor returns to her last night with Maestro and the fact that after all the wide and deep conversations and exchanges they had, about performances and revolutions and art and war, in buses and cars and cafes and restaurants, this is how things had to end between them. That a person she cannot help but consider a soulmate, a guiding light, a Maestro, ultimately became one more estranged travel companion all because of something as simple as a rejected kiss. Of course, Mi Amor knows that there is nothing simple about a kiss. Especially one that is rejected. Especially one that is rejected by a woman. A young woman. A young woman who acknowledges a connection with a man and still chooses to draw a line. No. Nothing simple about that.

Lights flicker.

From the desire to perfect a new tongue, to a realization that communication doesn't always require accuracy.

Mi Amor re-installs and de-installs and re-installs the letters.

Lights flicker.

Sometimes, when Mi Amor thinks of that farewell, she sees it as emblematic of her own misinterpretation. Of a surface-level relationship that she gave more importance than was due. The kind of connection that she misinterpreted as something beyond—as something spiritual and inexplicable while in reality it was nothing more or less than a man's pursuit of a sexual liaison with a young woman who admired him.

Lights flicker.

From a wish to understand every word and every nuance, to coming to terms with understanding enough.

Mi Amor re-installs and de-installs and re-installs the letters.

Lights flicker.

Sometimes, when she thinks of that farewell, Mi Amor sees it as representing the absolute futility of human engagement. The banality of how people come together and break apart. The ordinariness of interactions that each of us imbues with colour and life and vividness simply because we need to. Mi Amor was travelling alone. She was lonely. She was living in languages that were not hers. Seeing her connection to Maestro as something magical gave that period in Guatemala more significance. Knowing a guerrillera theatre maker infused her own revolutionary zest for an altered world. So perhaps that's all it was. An ordinary relationship that was seemingly extraordinary simply because of who Mi Amor was. At that moment. In that July.

Lights flicker.

From a searing need for all the letters to make sense, to accepting that she will forever be marked by them, regardless of their meaning.

Mi Amor re-installs and de-installs and re-installs the letters.

Lights flicker.

Sometimes, when Mi Amor thinks of that farewell, she thinks that perhaps it was the only way. The only way to make saying goodbye easier for both of them.

Perhaps they both knew that farewells that are said on the heels of a disagreement soften the emotional blow of separation.

Perhaps somewhere, consciously or subconsciously, both Maestro and Mi Amor knew that this would be a way to guard themselves from the lasting effects of a potentially life-altering relationship that circumstances would make transient.

Perhaps Maestro hyperbolized his reaction to Mi Amor's drunken kiss with another man and, in so doing, made it easier to say goodbye. For both of them.

Perhaps Maestro knew that the young woman who breezed into Guatemala with grandiose notions of understanding the role of theatre in times and places of war, was never going to walk the shores of Lake Atitlan again.

Lights down.

6 You

Part three

Now, think about the light. The light that's in that space with you, around you, within you. The light that might illuminate the entirety of the space or only parts of it. The light that creates shadows and that which negates it.

Ask yourself what kind of light exists in your creation, with you and your companions and your time. Ask yourself how it manifests. What kind of instrument produces the light? Does it have a shape? What colour is the light? Does the light have a physical body? Can walls, for example, be made of light? Maybe the light is the thing that connects your fragments. Maybe it is the light that gives your imagination some shape.

- you can write directly into the spaces provided
- you can write in a space of your choosing
- you can use the following link to engage with a collaborative, virtual space that has been created for the reader-writers of this book: https://tinyurl.com/WritinginBetween2. The same link can also be accessed by scanning the QR code

DOI: 10.4324/9781032685823-24

The process from here on out is an iterative one and all you need to do is go back and forth. Back and forth and back and forth and back and forth, considering always where the overlaps happen and the fractures. Where the connections happen and the breaks. Back and forth and back and forth and back and forth. Mixing and matching the versions of yourself that exist in this space that you've built, with the light you've imagined, in the particular time that you've chosen, alongside the versions of the person(s)/ idea(s)/ place(s) who are there with you.

One version of yourself in one kind of light, doing a specific thing, in one particular July with your chosen companion. Then the same version of yourself in another kind of light, doing something else, in a different July, with the same companion. Followed by the same but different version yourself in a third kind of light, doing the same thing as before, in a different July, with a different companion. Culminating with all versions of yourself and your chosen companion in the darkness of one last July, doing absolutely nothing.

The options are endless, really.

Back and forth.

You.

The light.
A kind of doing. Or un-doing.
A July.
A companion.
A July.
A kind of doing. Or redoing.
You.
The light.
Back and forth.
Till you're ready to stop.

- you can write directly into the spaces provided
- you can write in a space of your choosing
- you can use the following link to engage with a collaborative, virtual space that has been created for the reader-writers of this book: https://tinyurl.com/WritinginBetween2. The same link can also be accessed by scanning the QR code

7 Amma

Lights up.

Nandu is in a rectangular space that is composed of four very differently constructed walls.

One of the walls is made of books: Enid Blyton's fairy tales, Nancy Drew and Hardy Boys' case files, Mills and Boon romance novels, Chemistry textbooks, Math notes, Ayn Rand's musings, comic versions of the Ramayana and the Mahabharata.

Another wall is made of objects like Nandu's green, red, and gold Bharatanatyam costume, the harmonium that her music teacher uses, glass paints, a range of paint brushes; the joy Nandu feels when she dances, or her pride when she wins painting competitions.

A third wall is made of Nandu's ambitions: her dreams of taking over her father's business, of wanting to get a state rank in her tenth-grade exams, of meeting Sachin Tendulkar some day and getting him to fall in love with her.

The last wall has nothing on it at the moment. Perhaps a blank canvas. Perhaps invisible prison bars.

Within the walls of words and arts and dreams and the unknown, Nandu is practising steps she has learned in her dance class.

First speed: Thaaangidu ——tha ——tha ——dhi ——na
Thaaangidu ——tha ——tha ——dhi ——na
Thaaangidu ——tha ——tha ——dhi ——na
Thaaangidu ——tha ——tha ——dhi ——na
(X2)

DOI: 10.4324/9781032685823-25

This particular adavu involves sitting down on the floor, on her toes, for one second, before standing up on her toes in the next.

Second speed: Thaangidu ——tha ——tha ——dhi ——na
Thaangidu ——tha ——tha ——dhi ——na
Thaangidu ——tha ——tha ——dhi ——na
Thaangidu ——tha ——tha ——dhi ——na
(X2)

Down-up. Up-down, Down-up. Up-down.

Third speed: Thangidu—tha—tha—dhi—na
Thangidu—tha—tha—dhi—na
Thangidu—tha—tha—dhi—na
(X2)

This is Nandu's least favourite adavu.

Lights change.

July 1988. Coimbatore.

Nandu's childhood home that is named after her grandfather's flourishing business empire.

In the ground floor drawing room that has built-in sofas lining two walls and a statue of Buddha inset into one of the others, Nandu's Amma and one of her Amma's friends are swapping stories about their children over cups of tea and a large quantity and variety of snacks—Amma has a reputation of being one of the most generous and gracious hosts in all the city. Heck, in all of Tamil Nadu. Today, for example, alongside freshly made, just-the-right-temperature Brooke Bond tea, Amma has a range of offerings for her pal: a bowl of banana chips and a plate of mysore pak from Sri Krishna sweets and freshly baked fruit buns from Sun Star Bakery.

Amma: Those steps that they make them do in Bharatanatyam, it'll help her lose weight.

Amma's friend: She's three and a half years old. Why are you worrying about that now?

Amma: Come on, yaa. Toddlers can also be fat. You know, she was the biggest child in the ward when she came out. You should have seen . . . even the doctor was surprised . . . . I didn't gain any weight with her brother, but with her, even the pregnancy fat has been hard to get off.

Amma's friend: When have you ever been fat! Look at you.

Amma: No, no, I've put on one kilo. Weight has always been a problem for me . . . that's why I want her to be disciplined from now . . . . Illayna, by the time she's my age, God only knows. Here, have some more.

Amma is really worried about Nandu's appetite.

She knows that the multiple midnight feedings that her child demanded during the first nine months of her existence have already led to a mouth full of dental caries. Dental caries: that's the term the dentist uses to describe Nandu's teeth, which have rotted into black nubs—their condition attributed to several months of middle-of-the-night feeds after which her mother couldn't help but fall back into bed, exhausted, without having a chance to ensure that there was no milk residue stuck to her baby's emerging fangs.

Of course, as soon as she is given this information, Amma blames herself for not having paid enough attention to her child. She never thinks to ask why she is the one who has to wake up for every midnight feed. She never stops to consider if she might be less tired if her husband shared night shifts with her. She never pauses to question if the male dentist is shaping the narrative in a way that places the blame on no one else's shoulders but the mother's. This is a quality Amma has always had; she blames herself for her children's actions. However old they get, Amma wonders what she must have fucked up in her parenting style in order to have caused her children's inexplicable choices.

In the July of 1988 Amma is blaming herself more than usual because, on top of having black rotting teeth, Nandu is chubby. And if that isn't enough, the doctor has told Amma that from some initial calculations based on her growth patterns until that point, he estimates Nandu will be six feet tall.

Amma: And her brother?

Doctor: He'll probably be 5 feet 10 inches.

As the doctor tells her that, Amma imagines her daughter growing up to become a gigantic woman with no teeth, walking next to her much smaller-in-size brother who, beside his sister's frame, looks like a delicate flower. Amma imagines the way people will stare at her daughter. The way they will judge her. The way they will reject her when it comes time to find her a husband. The way Amma's mother had judged her.

For being too dark.

For being too fat.

For not wanting to wear hand-me-downs made from old curtains.

For not being as beautiful as her older sister.

For not having lustrous hair like her younger sister.

For not being born with her brother's sex.

As the doctor tells her that her daughter might grow taller than her son, Amma's imagination gets the better of her, and the first thing she does when she comes home is ask her husband to get a pull-up bar installed in the garden so that she can force Nandu's brother to hang every morning—he needs to be taller than his sister. Boys cannot be shorter than their female siblings. And once she thinks she has a solution for the height problem, and the dentist assures her that nature will ensure Nandu's black teeth fall out and become white pearls, Amma has only one problem to solve. She needs to get her daughter to lose weight.

So to kill two birds with one stone, Amma decides that Nandu needs to be enrolled in Bharatanatyam classes as soon as possible, at the age of three and a half. That way, not only will her daughter learn more about Indian culture, Amma tells herself—knowledge that will make an important addition to her daughter's resume for marriage—but Nandu will get the exercise that needs to work off all those calories she can't help but consume.

In the July of 1988, Amma is doing her research.

Amma: Who are the dance teachers around the area? I see . . . And she is reliable? . . . I see . . . She's new, though, right? . . . . Aama, it'll definitely be cheaper. Do you want your daughter to also want to take the classes? . . . Exactly; sharing the petrol costs would make it a lot cheaper.

Once Amma has made a plan for how to streamline her daughter's figure, she knows she has to make the costs seem manageable to the powers that control the family's coffers; the last thing Amma wants is for her husband and father-in-law to tell her that she is spending more money than she should be. After all, this is what the men of the house always say when Amma talks about wanting to do anything outside the home: like when she wanted to get a job as a teacher and put her post-graduate certificate in education to use, beyond her children.

It's never told to her viciously. It's not like the men force Amma with threats or abuse to prevent her from working. No, nothing like that. Instead, their statements are framed as simple logic. Just facts. Pros and cons. A cost benefit analysis.

Amma's father-in-law:	It's not that you can't work, it's just that people will speak ill of us if you do. They'll think that we're the kind of family that can't even afford to take care of our daughters-in-law. We can't have that.
Amma's husband:	It's not that you can't volunteer, it's just a question of the math. If the petrol costs are going to add up to so much, and you're not even going to be making that much money, then it . . . well, it just becomes a wasteful expenditure of money. You also want her to go to these dance classes . . . . there are those fees and fuel costs. We need to be careful, darling . . . Ask the girl to bring me some coffee. That flight was exhausting.

Soft power.

Insidious power.

The kind of power that is often hard to name or blame or vilify because it is not communicated in harsh tones or loud voices.

The kind of power in which violations and abuses are almost impossible to identify because they don't show up in any of the ways that are expected.

The kind of power that is often not deciphered until decades have passed, and a lifetime has gone by.

Amma's husband:	It was a horrible trip.
Amma:	Really? But I've heard that Singapore is such an exciting place.
Amma's husband:	Bullshit. Couldn't get good sambar anywhere and we were stuck in meetings all day. I wish we didn't have to go to these conferences. Such a waste of time.

Amma: Can I go with you next time?
Amma's husband: Why? I'm telling you, it's horrible, darling.
Amma: I just want to . . . you know . . . see . . .

In the July of 1988 Amma craves chances to see a world outside the handful of cities that she has visited in India. She wants to travel beyond the borders of her country and into foreign lands. She wants to experience new cultures and try new foods and buy new fabrics that she can fashion into funky, fusion-y kurtas that no one else is wearing. She wants to buy jewellery too; she has a penchant for gold and diamonds.

In the July of 1988, Amma finds herself daydreaming about her husband giving her the kinds of adventures that her grandmother couldn't think of wanting.

In the July of 1988, Amma finds herself daydreaming about her husband giving her the kinds of adventures that her mother couldn't think of having.

In the July of 1988, Mi Amma finds herself daydreaming about her husband giving her the kinds of adventures that she hopes Nandu will never have to depend on a man for.

Lights change.

Every time Amma has a conversation that keeps her confined to spaces defined by her husband or either of their families, every time social and cultural enactments of control keep her in her place, the borders around Nandu change.

First speed: *Thaaa ——thai ——thai ——tha*
Dhhhi ——thai ——thai ——tha
Thaaa ——thai ——thai ——tha
Dhhhi ——thai ——thai ——tha
(X2)

Every time Amma's freedoms are curtailed by what people will say and think and critique and judge, the space around her daughter grows.

Shifts.

Gains.

Second speed: *Thaa ——thai ——thai ——tha*
Dhhi ——thai ——thai ——tha
Thaa ——thai ——thai ——tha
Dhhi ——thai ——thai ——tha
(X2)

Almost as if the mother's every restriction contributes to her daughter's increasing freedom.

She doesn't notice it then of course; Nandu continues to dance and has no idea that her Amma's constraints are wound up in her liberties.

Amma is not always conscious of that either.

Third speed: *Tha—thai—thai—tha*
Dhi—thai—thai—tha
Tha—thai—thai—tha
Dhi—thai—thai—tha
(X2)

Lights change.

July 1995.

"What do you want to be when you grow up?"

Amma asks Nandu this question every so often, as often as she can remember to because she wants to ensure that her daughter dares to dream. Maybe she'll be a doctor (who is also a wife and a mother, of course). Or an engineer (who is also a wife and a mother). Or a chartered accountant (who is also a wife and a mother). Amma wants Nandu to have a job that pays money so that she'll never have to depend on a man financially (except for when being a good wife and mother require her to stay home—no job can be more important than that).

That being said, even though she doesn't want Nandu to be like her, even though Amma wants her daughter to study and work and travel and do all the things that Amma never got to do, she cannot help but feel a twinge of hurt when Nandu's answer to her question is never met with: "When I grow up, I want to be like you, Amma." Instead, Amma notices that Nandu's choices are informed by the men in her life: her grandfathers, her father, her uncles, her brother . . . Of course, Amma understands exactly why her daughter wants to be like the men. Amma understands, however much it stings each time Nandu makes a statement about wanting to be like her father or her grandfather or her uncle, why she does so. After all, the men are barely at home during the children's waking hours and so are very rarely involved in anything to do with the day-to-day banalities of their care. The men are the ones who pay for dinners and school excursions and dance classes and all the things of fun and luxury, while the women are the disciplinarians who tell the children to do their homework and wash their hair and wake up on time and finish the vegetables on their plate.

The men are the ones who have different outlets for discipline and judgment—their wives . . . . So yes, Amma completely understands why Nandu shapes her ambitions for the future in the image of what she sees as being possible for the men in her life. Especially her father.

Of course, this changes.

Nandu's ideas about who she wants to be, how she wants to be, eventually change.

Slowly.

Quickly.

Generally.

Specifically.

One afternoon in the July of 1995, as Nandu is changing out of her nightie and wearing nothing but her cotton petticoat, her dad tries to come into her room—for some banal reason—without knocking on the door. Reacting with the kind of instinct that can only be described as being ingrained in her from everything that she has heard and seen about Indian women needing to be careful about their bodies and who sees which parts of them, Nandu jumps at the turn of that doorknob so that she can shut the door before her father sees her in her current state of undress. His simultaneous pushing it open with her pushing it closed leads, inevitably, to a scratch on the door.

A pull. A push. A scrape. A scratch.

A pull.

A push.

A scrape.

A scratch.

Nothing more. Nothing less.

But that's all it takes for this to be the first time that Nandu sees her father losing his temper. The first time she sees, first-hand, the notorious temper that she has heard a lot about, from her brother. Her brother has told her, and she has have never believed him, that their father's temper could be paralyzing in its intensity. Her brother has told her, and she has never believed him, that their father's ire is something to be remembered for the ages. Nandu's brother has told her this, but she has never believed him because her father has never once lost his temper at her.

But today, in this July, a pull, a push, a scrape, and a scratch are all it takes to set him off.

Perhaps Nandu's father has had a bad day at the office. Or perhaps he has had another argument with his brother. Or perhaps he feels inadequate again. Or perhaps he is hungover. Or perhaps he is recovering from being jealous about Amma talking to a clearly flirtatious Lothario at the party the night before.

Whatever the case is, the hairline scratch on the door is all her father needs that day to show Nandu the temper that she has never seen before. And once the momentary fear that she will pee her pants passes, once Nandu catches her breath, for the first time in her young life, she is not sure she wants to be like her father at all.

Amma notices this, of course. She notices everything.

She notices how carefully Nandu watches as her father's emotions start to spiral, more and more out of his control, until he is finally diagnosed with a miscalibration of chemicals in his brain, which leads to both her parents having to live in a mental health treatment facility for a few months—away from their children—to get him the help he needs to become functional again.

She notices how intensely Nandu observes her father's changed behaviour when he returns from the facility. How romantic he has become toward his wife. How he buys her flowers and makes open declarations of love in a way he has never done before. "Your Amma saved my live, Nandu. She saved my life."

She notices how much like father his daughter is. In her work ethic. In her sense of humour. In her psychological make-up.

Amma notices all of this. She notices everything.

Lights change.

The rectangular borders around Nandu continue to change, and the blank wall that lies on one side of her slowly starts to take on attributes.

Opinions.

Ideas.

Things that Nandu cannot name just yet, but that soon come to define how she sees herself as being different from what she always thought—consciously or unconsciously—that she had to be.

First speed: *Thaaai ——hath ——thaaai ——hi*
Thaaai ——hath ——thaaai ——hi
Thaaai ——hath ——thaaai ——hi
Thaaai ——hath ——thaaai ——hi
(x2)

As the blank wall gets filled up bit by bit, Nandu continues to dance.

And read.
And paint.
And sing.
And write.
And study.
And think.
And take new classes, more classes in this.
And that.
And the other.

Second speed: *Thaai ——hath ——thaai ——hi*
Thaai ——hath ——thaai ——hi
Thaai ——hath ——thaai ——hi
Thaai ——hath ——thaai ——hi
(x2)

It's almost as if Nandu doesn't ever stand still. Almost as if she doesn't know how to.

Third speed: *Thai—hath—thai—hi*
Thai—hath—thai—hi
Thai—hath—thai—hi
Thai—hath—thai—hi
(x2)

Lights change.

July 2000.

Amma had started entering Nandu in dance competitions when she was four years old—kept doing so even when her daughter would, in the early years, run off stage, weeping, before her performance began. Never one to quit, Amma soon figured out that her daughter's anxiety eased when her mother was not in her line of sight. Somehow, knowing that Amma was watching and supporting her *invisibly*, made Nandu a better performer. Somehow, being able to see her mother's encouragement had the opposite effect. It will take Nandu a lifetime of therapy to figure that one out.

Nandu eventually gets over her stage fright, though, and Amma ensures that—before her fifteenth birthday—Nandu has taken part in keyboard lessons, fancy dress and dance competitions, badminton tournaments, quiz contests, talent shows, and temple festivals. Amma ensures that her daughter has had a range of opportunities in which to showcase her talents; talents that she has made sure to cultivate and encourage and support; talents that she has convinced and cajoled her husband to support financially; talents Amma wishes her own mother had helped her nurture in herself.

Perhaps it is no surprise then that by the July of 2000, Nandu has become intensely competitive and ambitious of her own accord. It isn't enough to be a dancer, she has to learn how to choreograph her own dances to music of different genres. It isn't enough to simply be a badminton player, she has to join the district team and be one of the best female players in her city. It isn't enough to simply do well in the tenth standard exams, she has to get a state rank. It isn't enough to go to a local high school for her junior and senior year, she must go to the new international, residential school outside the city of Pune—and she needs to make sure to get in with a full scholarship.

Nandu will never fully understand why she is this way. Why it is always about doing more and being more and achieving more. Why it is that, even when she eventually becomes more anti-establishment—many, many Julys later—conventional recognition matters. Why it is that she feels this burning ache to keep pushing herself the day, the hour, the minute after one achievement has been garnered. Does it all go back to how she was pushed, as a child, to try every possible class and workshop and contest and competition? Does it all go back to how her Amma raised her, from the time she was three, to keep exploring everything that her body and mind were capable of?

Or had she simply been born this way, giving her Amma no choice but to look for avenues with which to satisfy her daughter's voracious appetites?

Amma:	I knew it. As soon as she got into the interview round, I knew she would get admission.
Amma's mother-in-law:	You should have never let her apply.
Amma:	Your son was the one who forced me. I never agreed.
Amma's husband:	She'll get to study in the U.S. if she goes to this school . . . And she has a scholarship. How can we not let her go?
Amma:	She's too young to go to a boarding school.
Amma's husband:	We let her brother go to boarding school when he was seven!
Amma's mother-in-law:	I didn't agree with that either.
Amma:	It's different for a boy.

Silence.

Nandu: I really want to do this. I want to go. I loved the place.

Silence.

Amma:	Did you see all the other girls there? Wearing shorts . . . . Mudila dyea . . . . That other girl from Kerala . . . what was her name? Did you see her hair was green in colour? She'll go there, and she'll become all westernized, and then it'll be your fault.
Amma's husband:	This is the kind of education I wish I had had. I want her to have it.
Amma's mother-in-law:	What was wrong with your education?
Amma's husband:	Nothing was wrong with it, Amma. Patshay, I wanted to go to the U.S., ormay ondo? Acha said no.
Amma's mother-in-law:	So? You turned out just fine.

Pause.

Amma's husband: This is her education. We are not going to stand in her way.

Amma might have been the one to cultivate Nandu's ambition, but now that she sees its fruit, this mother is no longer certain that she has done the right thing. She had always thought that her efforts would result in a talented, well-rounded, smart young woman who would do well in school, go to college, and find a well-paying job before getting married. In Amma's imagination, Nandu's success meant her not being dependent on a man financially; it meant her not living in a joint family set up like the one Amma had been married into; it meant Nandu not having to ask for anyone's approval in decisions that were made about the raising of her future children. These were the dreams that Amma had when she had pushed her daughter to be a great student and a wonderful dancer and a decent athlete and a painter and a singer and and and and. Never in her wildest imagination, however, did Amma think that all this cultivation of talent would lead to her daughter being able to get admission into a school that was two days away by train. Never in all her dreaming for her daughter did Amma want for her girl child to leave home at the age of fifteen, with a view toward attending university in an entirely different country—that was all her husband's doing.

So, in the July of 2000, when Nandu is packing her bags to leave for her last two years of high school in a town far, far away, Amma is heartbroken. Her friends don't understand how she could possibly let her daughter do this. "Did she fail her tenth standard exams? Do you have to send her there?" they ask, incredulous that any parent in a family that values Indian culture would consider sending a girl to live outside the home as an adolescent.

Beginning in the July of 2000 Amma's crises of faith in her parenting begins to take root, and as the Julys pass, her fears and regrets and disappointments only keep growing:

When she drops Nandu off at her new school and realizes that boys live in the dorm room that is right next door to her daughter's, and one of these male residents walks out of the shower at the very moment that Amma looks over, wearing nothing but a towel.

When her daughter calls home a few months after July 2000 to say that she has fallen in love and wants to bring home a boyfriend. A white boy. With piercings.

When the almost sixteen-year-old Nandu brings this boy home and doesn't seem all that troubled by her parents' threats. "I cut off ties with my brother," her father tells her, "If you upset your Amma, I'll cut off ties with you" (of course, Nandu is far from being unfazed; she remains scarred by her father's warning for most of her adult life).

Starting in the July of 2000, Amma and Nandu's relationship takes a devastating hit. From one in which mother and daughter had a connection based on honesty and trust and encouragement to one in which secrets start being kept; one in which each views the other with scepticism and regret and, worst of all, distrust. Amma is broken-hearted that she cannot trust her daughter to embody the values that she has worked so hard to instil in her. Nandu is heartbroken that whenever she tries to embody the honesty her mother taught her, she is met with nothing but recrimination, judgment, and something close to disgust.

"This is all your father's fault. We should never have let you leave home that young."

The cycle of angst between this mother and daughter repeats itself over and over and over again after the July of 2000:

When Nandu decides to accept an offer to study in the United States.
When she doesn't visit India as much as her mother wants her too.
When she keeps turning down Amma's offers to set her up with eligible men.
When she doesn't deny the possibility of loving people who are not men.
When she decides to study theatre.
When she says she is open to kissing someone on stage if the role demands it.
When she wants to travel to countries that Amma hasn't heard of.
When she speaks about ideals of "changing the world" rather than "making a family."
When she talks about wanting to work in war zones.
"When will your ambition finish?" Amma asks Nandu in a July not long after that of 2000.
"Is ambition something that can finish, Amma? Weren't you the one who taught me to always keep pushing myself?"
Oh yes. Amma really regrets her parenting choices now.

Lights change.

The walls of the rectangular structure around Nandu start to shift. Evolve. Adapt.

Thana——dhiiirana——dhirana——thana ——dhiiirana

No longer is there only one wall made of books; that wall has acquired two or three additional walls of more books—academic books; books she has written; books she plans to write—that lie parallel with the first one.

Thana——dhiiirana——dhirana——thana ——dhiiirana

Additional walls of artistic artefacts rise up parallel to the art-infused wall that stood before; the new ones equally interspersed with notions of changing the world through creative pursuits as they are realistic artefacts that reflect Nandu's newfound passion for the theatre.

Thana ——dhiirana ——dhirana ——thana ——dhiirana

There are more ambition walls that emerge too, of course, parallel with the first one that contains Nandu's childhood dreams: new ones that document her shifting career goals for herself (from being a doctor to a reporter to a celebrity to a chartered accountant to an entrepreneur to an investment banker to an economist to a social worker to an artist to to to to to . . .); new walls that record her shifting personal goals for herself (from having a first crush to a first love to a second love to a next love to not believing in the institution of marriage to long distance relationships to considering polyamory to to to to . . .)

Thana —dhiirana —dhirana —thana —dhiirana

And not to be left out of the additional walls that the others have gained, the fourth wall—the one that used to be blank—gains a number of parallel walls too. Newly blank. Newly ripe with potential for all Nandu's ideas that remain to be imagined and birthed and evolved.

Thana—dhirana—dhirana—thana—dhirana

The walls add and add and add to themselves and make the structures around Nandu more expansive.

More claustrophobic.

Thana—dhirana—dhirana—thana—dhirana

Lights change.

July 2005—July 2014.

Amma is delighted when her daughter visits her childhood home after her first visit to Uganda—Nandu's first visit to an active war zone. The kind of visit that shakes a person to their very core and makes them grapple with what it means to be human. What it means to be themselves. The kind of life-altering-ness that leads to Nandu not being able to think of much beyond her time in northern Uganda.

Of the stories she has heard.

Of the people she has met.

Of the sparks that have been ignited.

Of the journeys that remain to be had.

Of the work that is left to be done.

Nandu is so caught up in her discoveries about theatre and war and everything related to it that she has almost forgotten that this is the first time she is entering her home after her grandmother's death. A death that had occurred while she was staying at a dingy motel on top of a bar in Lira, which repeatedly played Kenny Rogers' "The Gambler" on repeat. A peaceful death during slumber that seemed more manageable and less shattering because it had happened while she was in a context where people who were much younger and much healthier were being killed for no fault of theirs. A context in which the sound of broken bottles in drunken bar brawls below where she slept made her fear that gunshots were being fired. A context in which signing a waiver absolving her hosts of responsibility should something happen to her in an IDP camp seemed like she was signing her life away. In the context of the kinds of things that people were living and dying through in northern Uganda, hearing that her 70-something-old grandmother with multiple health issues had died in her sleep was news that Nandu is able to handle with something akin to grace.

In the July of 2005, when Nandu returns home after her first time in an active war zone, she is so caught up in her epiphanies and discoveries and realizations that she doesn't really get into what the matriarch's loss means for their home. What it means to the man—the same man that Nandu shares an undeniable connection with—who had been married to her grandmother for over five decades. What it means to her older son, who is now almost as infirm as his mother was during her last days. What it means to her younger son, Nandu's father, who was just as much the apple of his mother's eye as he was constantly struggling with feeling second to his older brother in the extent of her affection. Nandu's grandmother's death meant many things to many people, perhaps most of all, to Amma.

Sometimes, Nandu's grandmother was the patronizing mother-in-law who earned Amma's anger with parenting tips that the latter thought the former was in no position to offer (her sons were both spoiled brats, after all).

Sometimes, Nandu's grandmother was the woman who rubbed Amma the wrong way by very obviously showing her preference for her male grandchildren (Nandu's brother was always her preferred grandchild, and she made no secret of it).

Sometimes, Nandu's grandmother was Amma's unconditional support system (the way she took care of Nandu and her brother when Amma and her younger son had to live at the mental health facility).

Sometimes, she was Amma's favourite source of gossip (she would relay all the goings on at her older son's house after the ties between the brothers were cut off and the men's wives and children weren't allowed to directly communicate with each other).

Sometimes, she was the amazing chef who would share recipes while making sure to leave out the most crucial ingredient so that her daughter-in-law could never recreate her magic in the kitchen (mutton biriyani; steam pudding; mariappan rolls; rainbow sandwiches; ginger chicken; mutton cutlets—these were some of her specialities).

All the time, she was someone that Amma cared for diligently, especially when her septuagenarian body started to fail her, and her two sons were not in any physical or emotional state to take care of her (her older son was paralyzed from a stroke; her younger one was in the midst of a third relapse of depression).

In the July of 2005, Nandu is so caught up in her own shit that she doesn't know how to understand what Amma has lost and gained with the departure of her mother-in-law.

In the July of 2005, Nandu doesn't understand the intricacies of grief.

She won't until many Julys later. Much after this July of 2005 that marks her grandmother's death.

In the July of 2005, Nandu doesn't understand the intricacies of her Amma's various obvious and less obvious griefs, and it will take her a lifetime to unravel even a small number of their intersections. There are the griefs that Amma wears visibly—like the loss of her mother-in-law; like having to watch her husband go through the torments of mental illness; like having both her children leave home much younger than she would have liked them to. And then there are the griefs that are less visible, less obvious, perhaps even to Amma herself. Is there a grief that comes from not having had a say in who she was married off to, even when love was eventually found with that person? Is there a grief that comes from having been sent to her husband's home to live with his family, where she didn't feel fully understood? Is there a grief that sets in when she is told that she cannot pursue her desires to work or travel? A grief that never goes way because of a child that was lost before the ones that were born?

Nandu might never understand the sheer range of Amma's griefs because the latter's grieving, most of the time, doesn't look like grief. In the Julys of 2006 and 2007 and 2008 and 2009 and 2010 and and and and and . . . , Amma's grief constantly manifests as anger toward her children and their choices. An anger that shows itself in fights that she picks with Nandu. An anger that Nandu initially sees as nothing more or less than an unreasonable mother. An anger that Amma's daughter only knows to nuance sometime in the July of 2014, months after their relationship has taken another beating because of the way in which Amma decides to organize Nandu's wedding: an event for the ages that Amma sees as being hers, rather than her daughter's; a wedding that is celebrated in all the ways that Nandu does not want.

Amma: I regret the day your father sent you to that school. I told him. I said, "It's all your fault your daughter has turned out like this."

Nandu: What has that got to do with any of this?

Amma: Everything. That's when you started becoming all . . . like this. How could you not know that you need to stand up at a wedding reception when the guests come to congratulate you? How could any Indian girl not know that?

Nandu: I honestly didn't know.

Amma: I don't believe you.

Nandu: Are you seriously accusing me of . . . I don't know . . . what are you accusing me of, Ma?

Amma: I worked so hard to make my—your—wedding a successful celebration, and you are just determined to spoil everything. You've been sad and morose the entire time . . . Endha nyan chaidhada? All I tried to do was give you the kind of wedding that people in Coimbatore will be talking about for years. The kind of wedding that I wish my mother had given me.

Nandu: I'm not you! You did everything I specifically asked you not to do. All I wanted was a quiet ceremony and for you to donate all that money you spent to t—

Amma: —again with that donation nonsense. Why should I donate the money to some scholarship fund? Why should I care about some other child's education? I care about *my* child. I care about *my* child's wedding . . . "All I wanted," she says; utter nonsense. What kind of wedding would it have been if I followed your requests? Ninda ideas . . . . ellam avadayaana thodangiyadha.

Nandu: Come on, Ma. You can't blam —

Amma: I can do whatever I like.

Nandu and Amma don't talk to each other after the former's wedding ends in Bollywood style family drama. They don't talk for days. Weeks. A time during which everyone in their family tries their hand at getting mother and daughter to mend the damage. Amma's brother calls Nandu, weeping on the phone, begging her to make things right with his sister. Nandu's brother calls his younger sibling, asking her to be diplomatic—for once—instead of speaking her mind. Nandu's bemused and slightly appalled at his new family's emotional-drama husband calls his mother-in-law and tries to mend fences in a way that only a new son-in-law can. Nandu's father tries to calm his wife down, reminding her that she couldn't be upset with her daughter for not enjoying a wedding that had been conducted in all the ways that the latter had requested for it not to be. Of course, he is met with "This is all your fault. I told you we should have never sent her to that school."

After having had some form of contact almost every day, not speaking for weeks after the wedding was extremely unusual for this mother and daughter. And given the sharpness of this fracture, it takes Amma and Nandu months, even years, to return to some semblance of normal.

Months, maybe years, for Amma to move past the hurt of not being appreciated by her daughter.

Months, maybe years, for Nandu to move past the hurt of not being understood by her mother.

It is only after the July of 2014, after Nandu moves away from India once more, that she begins to gain some sense of perspective. The kind of perspective that only time and distance can allow. The kind of perspective that allows her to see that maybe all her Amma's anger and angst and rage and seeming unreasonable-ness are nothing more or less than different manifestations of grief.

Grief at having raised a daughter who does not fit the norms of what good parenting should result in.

Grief for all the experiences that Nandu gets to have, that Amma was never even given the chance to consider for herself.

Grief for the people who have been lost and the paths that have gone unexplored.

Grief at what Amma once thought being a mother would be like and what it is like for her.

Lights change.

Both Amma and Nandu find themselves standing by each other in that confined area between the walls and each of their many layers.

Naaa ——dhru ——di ——thaaani

Thooom ——thru ——dhi ——thaaani

Dheeem ——thanadhirana

They don't say very much.

They don't do very much.

Whether or not they want to, mother and daughter aren't very good at asking each other the questions that need to be asked, or at listening in the ways the other needs.

Naaathru ——thillana

Thooomthru ——thillana

Udhanakatara ——dhiiiim ——dhim

But as they stand in that demarcated space that keeps them together and apart through many Julys that follow, they will come to learn that that they will always be intricately connected to each other's spaces. Those that are walled off. And those that are open.

Naa —dhru —di —thaani

Thoom —thru —dhi —thaani

Dheem —thanadhirana

Whether or not they want to, Nandu and her Amma will come to learn in many, many Julys, that however far they live from each other—geographically, temporally, ideologically, politically, philosophically—they will be inexplicably connected: in their embodiments of freedom and containment; in their understanding of togetherness and isolation; in their longing for each other in moments of unadulterated grief and inexplicable joy.

Naathru —thillana

Thoomthru —thillana

Udhanakatara —dhiiim —dhim

Almost without their consent, almost as if their bodies move before their minds can understand the movement that is being performed, Amma and Nandu start to dance. A thillana. A particular Bharatanatyam piece that marks the end of a longer dance recital. A piece that both mother and daughter had learned more than three decades apart; in different decades; in different cities; in different childhoods.

Na—dhru—di—thani

Thom—thru—dhi—thani

Dhem—thanadhirana

Thillanas are spirited, dynamic, fast-paced works of choreography that when performed in duos, require intricate collaborations that—to an uneducated eye—seem easy. There is nothing simple about these duets, though. Coordinating with a partner in a thillana requires multiple efforts: an eye needs to be on the partner; an ear needs to be tuned in to the beat that marks the next move; the body needs to use all the adrenaline it has gained from the much longer pieces that came before the thillana so that it can push itself over the finish line for the many thangidu-tha-tha-dhi-nas that seems to always find their way into this dance's script.

Nathru—thillana

Thomthru—thillana

Udhanakatara—dhiim—dhim

As mother and daughter move, sometimes in beautiful synchronicity and sometimes in obvious discord, the walls that stand around them—the walls that have walls that have walls—start reverberating with the beat of their naked feet on the ground. The walls that have walls that have walls start to shake as the mridangam increases in intensity, as Amma and Nandu start to move faster and faster and faster and faster. As Amma and Nandu finish their thillana, the walls that have walls that have walls shake and tremble and quiver and spasm but never fall.

Nadhrudithani

Thomthrudhithani

Dhemthanadhirana

Nathruthillana

Thomthruthillana

Udhanakataradhiimdhim

As soon as the piece ends, as soon as the last note is heard, these two connected yet discordant partners freeze for what feels like a second. A moment of respite. Rest. Quiet.

But before they can sink into it, before mother and daughter can truly immerse themselves in that calm,

Naaa ———dhru ———di ———

The dance begins.

Again.

Lights down.

8 You

The last part

By the time you stop, you'll probably have something messy.

A messy something that allows you a window into worlds you've always wanted to think about. More extensively. More rigorously. Differently.

A messy something that is nothing more or less than an evocative walk down the twists and turns of your memory and imagination.

A messy something that you want to work and rework so that it can reveal the form that you suspect to be lurking somewhere beneath the surface.

A messy something that just is.

Something that you might choose to share with the world.

Something that you might choose to destroy.

Something that you might choose to keep, just for yourself.

Your reality.

Your imagination.

Your July.

DOI: 10.4324/9781032685823-26

Section 4

Between writing and us

Question 1

How do our Safars in **F for** _____ ***perform a quest to make the political, personal?***

- you can write directly into the spaces provided
- you can write in a space of your choosing
- you can use the following link to engage with a collaborative, virtual space that has been created for the reader-writers of this book: https://tinyurl.com/WritinginBetween3. The same link can also be accessed by scanning the QR code

DOI: 10.4324/9781032685823-27

Question 2

How do our texts in* Julys *perform a quest to make the personal, political?

- you can write directly into the spaces provided
- you can write in a space of your choosing
- you can use the following link to engage with a collaborative, virtual space that has been created for the reader-writers of this book: https://tinyurl.com/WritinginBetween3. The same link can also be accessed by scanning the QR code

Question 3

If the meaning of "in between," performative writing might be fostered through collaboration, how do you envision the next stage in the evolution of this co-created form?

- you can write directly into the spaces provided
- you can write in a space of your choosing
- you can use the following link to engage with a collaborative, virtual space that has been created for the reader-writers of this book: https://tinyurl.com/WritinginBetween3. The same link can also be accessed by scanning the QR code

Index

For Product Safety Concerns and Information please contact our EU representative GPSR@taylorandfrancis.com
Taylor & Francis Verlag GmbH, Kaufingerstraße 24, 80331 München, Germany

www.ingramcontent.com/pod-product-compliance
Lightning Source LLC
Chambersburg PA
CBHW051748230426
43670CB00012B/2203
* 9 7 8 1 0 3 2 6 8 5 8 1 6 *